JAPANESE
in 10 minutes a day®

by **Kristine Kershul**, M.A., University of California, Santa Barbara

adapted by Linda Suyama Azuma

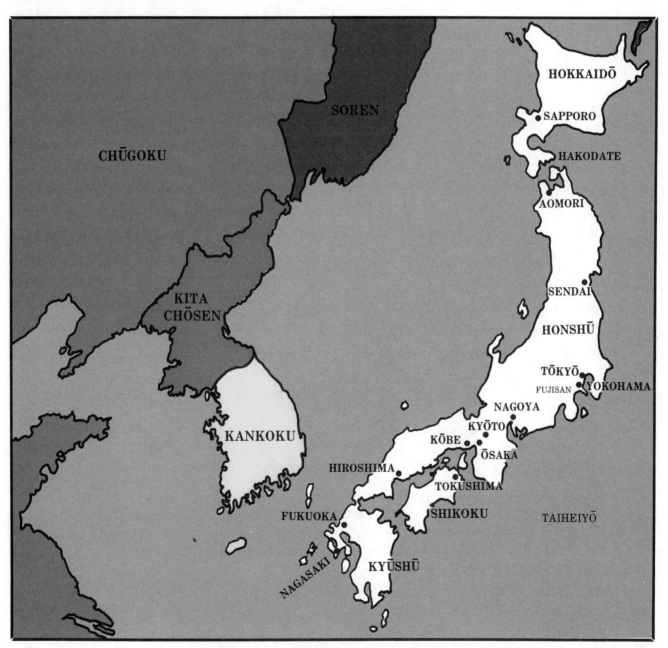

A Sunset Series

Lane Publishing Co.
Menlo Park, CA 94025

Second printing November 1988

Many Japanese letters sound the same as they do in English, but some Japanese letters are pronounced or written differently. To learn the Japanese sounds of these letters, write each example in the space provided, in addition to saying the word many times. After you practice the word, see if you can locate it on the map.

Japanese sound	English sound	Example	Write it here
a	ah	**Akasaka** *(ah-kah-sah-kah)*	_____
ā	āh *(elongated)*	**Denmāku** *(den-māh-koo)* Denmark	_____
ai	i *(as in pie)*/eye	**Sendai** *(sen-die)*	_____
e	eh *(as in let)*	**Kōbe** *(kōh-beh)*	_____
ē	ēh *(elongated)*	**Nōruwē** *(nōh-doo-wēh)* Norway	_____
ei	ay *(as in day)*	**Beikoku** *(bay-koh-koo)* America	_____
i	ee	**Hitachi** *(hee-tah-chee)*	_____
ii	ēē *(elongated)*	**Niigata** *(nēē-gah-tah)*	_____
o	oh	**Otaru** *(oh-tah-doo)*	_____
ō	ōh *(elongated)*	**Tōkyō** *(tōh-kyōh)*	_____
oi	oy *(as in boy)*	**Oita** *(oy-tah)*	_____
u	oo	**Fuji** *(foo-jee)*	_____
ū	ōō *(elongated)*	**Kyūshū** *(kyōō-shōō)*	_____

(wah)(gah)(oh)(nee)   (toh)

NOTES: • In Japanese, **wa, ga, o, ni** and **to** are some examples of "particle words." Oftentimes, "particle words" cannot be translated into English. When they have no English equivalents, these "particle words" will simply be marked (P).

• In Japanese, the letter "r" is never emphasized. It is pronounced like a soft "d."

• The letter "g" is always pronounced like the "g" in "go."

• A bar over a vowel in Japanese means to hold the sound a little longer.

Now practice the important words you learned on the inside front cover.

(nahn) (dess)   (kah)
Nan desu ka? _____
what   is it

(sah-keh)(dess)
Sake desu. _____
rice wine   it is

(sah-keh)(oh)(koo-dah-sigh)
Sake o kudasai. _____
rice wine   please give me

When you arrive in **Nihon,** *(nee-hohn)* / Japan the very first thing you will need to do is ask questions —

"Where is the train station?" "Where can I exchange money?" "Where **(doko)** *(doh-koh)* is the

lavatory?" "**Doko** *(doh-koh)* / where is a restaurant?" "**Doko** do I catch a taxi?" "**Doko** is a good hotel?"

"**Doko** is my luggage?" — and the list will go on and on for the entire length of your visit.

In Japanese, there are EIGHT KEY QUESTION WORDS to learn. These eight **tango** *(tahn-goh)* / words will

help you know exactly what you are ordering in a restaurant before you order it and not

after the surprise (or shock!) arrives. These **tango** *(tahn-goh)* / words are extremely important, so learn them

now. Take a few minutes to study and practice saying the eight basic question **tango** *(tahn-goh)* listed

below. Then cover the Japanese **tango** with your hand and fill in each of the blanks with

the matching Japanese **tango.** *(tahn-goh)* / word

1.	**DOKO** *(doh-koh)*	=	WHERE	*doko, doko*
2.	**NAN/NANI** *(nahn) (nah-nee)*	=	WHAT	_____
3.	**DARE** *(dah-deh)*	=	WHO	_____
4.	**DŌSHITE/NAZE** *(dōh-shtay) (nah-zeh)*	=	WHY	_____
5.	**ITSU** *(ee-tsoo)*	=	WHEN	_____
6.	**DŌ/IKAGA** *(dōh) (ee-kah-gah)*	=	HOW	_____
7.	**IKURA** *(ee-koo-dah)*	=	HOW MUCH	_____
8.	**IKUTSU** *(ee-koo-tsoo)*	=	HOW MANY	_____

Now test yourself to see if you really can keep these **tango** *(tahn-goh)* _{words} straight in your mind. Draw lines between the Japanese **to** *(toh)* _{and} English equivalents below.

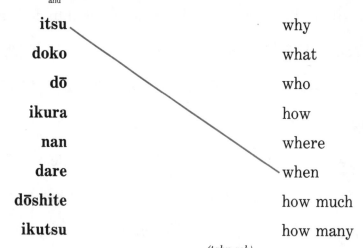

itsu	why
doko	what
dō	who
ikura	how
nan	where
dare	when
dōshite	how much
ikutsu	how many

(itsu connects to when)

Examine the following questions containing these **tango** *(tahn-goh)* _{words}. Practice the sentences out loud and then quiz yourself by filling in the blanks below with the correct question **tango.**

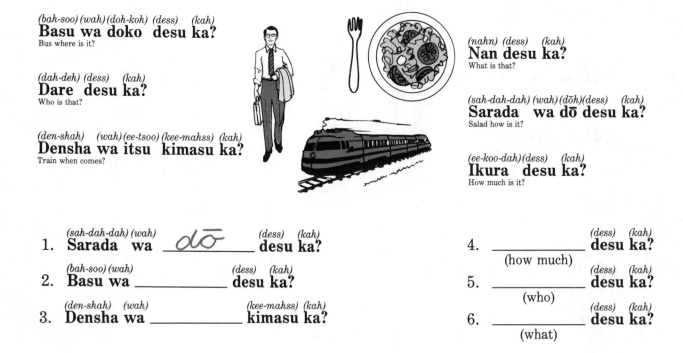

(bah-soo) (wah) (doh-koh) (dess) (kah)
Basu wa doko desu ka?
Bus where is it?

(dah-deh) (dess) (kah)
Dare desu ka?
Who is that?

(den-shah) (wah) (ee-tsoo) (kee-mahss) (kah)
Densha wa itsu kimasu ka?
Train when comes?

(nahn) (dess) (kah)
Nan desu ka?
What is that?

(sah-dah-dah) (wah) (dōh) (dess) (kah)
Sarada wa dō desu ka?
Salad how is it?

(ee-koo-dah) (dess) (kah)
Ikura desu ka?
How much is it?

1. *(sah-dah-dah) (wah)* **Sarada wa** _dō_ *(dess) (kah)* **desu ka?**

2. *(bah-soo) (wah)* **Basu wa** _____ *(dess) (kah)* **desu ka?**

3. *(den-shah) (wah)* **Densha wa** _____ *(kee-mahss) (kah)* **kimasu ka?**

4. _____ *(dess) (kah)* **desu ka?**
   (how much)

5. _____ *(dess) (kah)* **desu ka?**
   (who)

6. _____ *(dess) (kah)* **desu ka?**
   (what)

Doko *(doh-koh)* _{where} will be your most used question **tango,** *(tahn-goh)* _{word} so let's concentrate on it. Say each of the **Nihongo** *(nee-hohn-goh)* _{Japanese} sentences aloud many times. Then write out each sentence without looking at the example. If you don't succeed on the first try, don't give up. Just practice each sentence until you are able to do it easily. Don't forget that you pronounce **"r"** like a soft "d." Also

4 desu is usually pronounced "dess," **masu** is most often "mahss," and **"i"** is always "ee."

(toy-deh) (wah) (doh-koh) (dess) (kah)
Toire wa doko desu ka?
lavatory (P)
トイレ

MEN   WOMEN

(tah-koo-shēē) (wah) (doh-koh) (dess) (kah)
Takushii wa doko desu ka?
taxi (P)
タクシー

(bah-soo) (dess)
Basu wa doko desu ka?
bus (P)
バ ス

_____   _____   *Basu wa doko desu ka?*

(dess-toh-dahn) (doh-koh) (dess)
Resutoran wa doko desu ka?
restaurant (P)
レストラン

(geen-kōh) (dess)
Ginkō wa doko desu ka?
bank (P)
銀 行

(hoh-teh-doo) (dess)
Hoteru wa doko desu ka?
hotel
ホテル

_____   _____   _____

(tahn-goh)   **(ay-goh)**   **(nee-hohn-goh)**
Yes, many of the **tango** that look like **Eigo** are also **Nihongo.** Since **Nihongo** has adopted
English   Japanese

(ay-goh) (noh) (tahn-goh)
some **Eigo no tango,** your work here is simpler. You will be amazed at the number of
English (P) words

(tahn-goh)
tango that are very similar. Of course, they do not always sound the same when spoken in

Japanese, but the similarities will certainly help you. Listed below are five "free" **tango**
(tahn-goh)

beginning with "a" to help you get started. Be sure to say each **tango** aloud and then

(nee-hohn-goh) (tahn-goh)
write out the **Nihongo no tango** in the blank to the right.
Japanese (P) word

☑ **airon** *(eye-dohn)*	iron	_____
☑ **aisu hokkē** *(eye-soo) (hohk-kēh)*	ice hockey	_____
☑ **aisu kuriimu** *(eye-soo) (koo-dēē-moo)*	ice cream	_____
☑ **aisu sukēto** *(eye-soo) (soo-kēh-toh)*	ice skating	_____
☑ **Amerika** *(ah-meh-dee-kah)*	America	*amerika*

Free **tango** like these will appear at the bottom of the following pages in a yellow color

band. You don't have to work hard to learn them. They are easy — enjoy them!

Step 2

(koh-noh) *(soh-noh)* *(ah-noh)*
Kono, Sono, Ano
this   that   that over there

Like Chinese, **Nihongo** *(nee-hohn-goh)* does not have **tango** *(tahn-goh)* for "the" and "a." Instead **kono** *(koh-noh)*, **sono** *(soh-noh)* and **ano** *(ah-noh)* are used. These **tango** reflect the object's distance from the speaker.

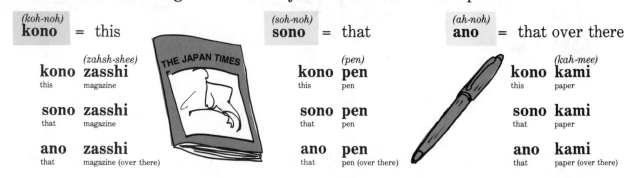

kono *(koh-noh)* = this   **sono** *(soh-noh)* = that   **ano** *(ah-noh)* = that over there

kono zasshi *(zahsh-shee)* (this magazine)	**kono pen** *(pen)* (this pen)	**kono kami** *(kah-mee)* (this paper)
sono zasshi (that magazine)	**sono pen** (that pen)	**sono kami** (that paper)
ano zasshi (that magazine (over there))	**ano pen** (that pen (over there))	**ano kami** (that paper (over there))

Nihongo has "measure words" for everything. **Mai** *(my)* is used with words like paper and stamps. **Hon** *(hohn)* (long, cylindrical) is used with words like pen and pencil. **Satsu** *(sah-tsoo)* (bound together) is used with words like book and magazine.

(nee) (sah-tsoo) (zahsh-shee)
ni satsu no zasshi
two (M) (P) magazines

(nee) (hohn) (pen)
ni hon no pen
(M) (P) pens

(my) (kah-mee)
ni mai no kami
(M) (P) paper

(yohn) (sah-tsoo) (zahsh-shee)
yon satsu no zasshi
four (M) (P) magazines

(hohn) (pen)
yon hon no pen
(M) (P) pens

(my) (kah-mee)
yon mai no kami
(M) (P) paper

Throughout **kono hon** *(hohn)*, "measure words" will be marked (M).

Step 3

(moh-noh)
Mono
things

Before you proceed with this Step, situate yourself comfortably in your living room. Now look around you. Can you name the **mono** *(moh-noh)* (things) that you see in this **heya** *(heh-yah)* (room) in **Nihongo?** *(nee-hohn-goh)* (Japanese) You can probably guess **sofā** *(soh-fah)* (sofa) and maybe even **tēburu** *(tēh-boo-doo)* (table). But let's learn the rest of them. After practicing these **tango** *(tahn-goh)* (words) out loud, write them in the blanks below and on the next page.

(eh)
e = (the) picture   *ℓ, ℓ, ℓ, ℓ, ℓ, ℓ*

(ten-jōh)
tenjō = (the) ceiling   _____

☐ **apāto** *(ah-pāh-toh)* .... apartment
☐ **appuru pai** *(ahp-poo-doo) (pie)* .... apple pie
☐ **anaunsā** *(ah-noun-sāh)* .... announcer
☐ **arubamu** *(ah-doo-bah-moo)* .... album
☐ **asuparagasu** *(ah-soo-pah-dah-gah-soo)*... asparagus

(kah-doh) **kado**	= (the) corner	_____	
(mah-doh) **mado**	= (the) window	_____	
(dahn-poo) **ranpu**	= (the) lamp	_____	
(den-tōh) **dentō**	= (the) light	_____	
(soh-fāh) **sofā**	= (the) sofa	_____	
(ee-soo) **isu**	= (the) chair	*isu, isu, isu*	
(kāh-pet-toh) **kāpetto**	= (the) carpet	_____	
(tēh-boo-doo) **tēburu**	= (the) table	_____	
(doh-ah) **doa**	= (the) door	_____	
(toh-kay) **tokei**	= (the) clock	_____	
(kāh-ten) **kāten**	= (the) curtain	_____	
(kah-beh) **kabe**	= (the) wall	_____	

Remember **Nihongo** *(nee-hohn-goh)* [Japanese] does not have words for "the" and "a." Now open your **hon** *(hohn)* [book] to the first page with the stick-on labels. Peel off the first 14 labels and proceed around the **heya,** *(heh-yah)* [room] labeling these items in your home. This will help to increase your **Nihongo** *(nee-hohn-goh)* word power easily. Don't forget to say the **tango** *(tahn-goh)* [word] as you attach each label.

Now ask yourself, "**E** *(eh)* [picture] **wa** *(wah)* [(P)] **doko** *(doh-koh)* [where] **desu** *(dess)* [is] **ka?** *(kah)*" and point at it while you answer, "**E** *(eh)* [picture] **wa** *(wah)* [(P)] **soko** *(soh-koh)* [there] **desu.** *(dess)* [is]" Continue on down the list until you feel comfortable with these new **tango.** *(tahn-goh)* [words] Say, "**Tenjō** *(ten-jōh)* [ceiling] **wa** *(wah)* [(P)] **doko** *(doh-koh)* [where] **desu** *(dess)* [is] **ka?**" Then reply, "**Tenjō** *(ten-jōh)* [ceiling] **wa** [(P)] **soko** *(soh-koh)* [there] **desu,** *(dess)* [is]" and so on.

When you can identify all the **mono** on the list, you will be ready to move on.

Now, starting on the next page, let's learn some basic parts of the house.

☐ **badominton** *(bah-doh-meen-tohn)*	badminton	_____
☐ **banana** *(bah-nah-nah)*	banana	_____
☐ **basukettobōru** *(bah-soo-ket-toh-bōh-doo)* . . .	basketball	_____
☐ **basu** *(bah-soo)*	bus	_____
☐ **bata** *(bah-tah)*	butter	_____

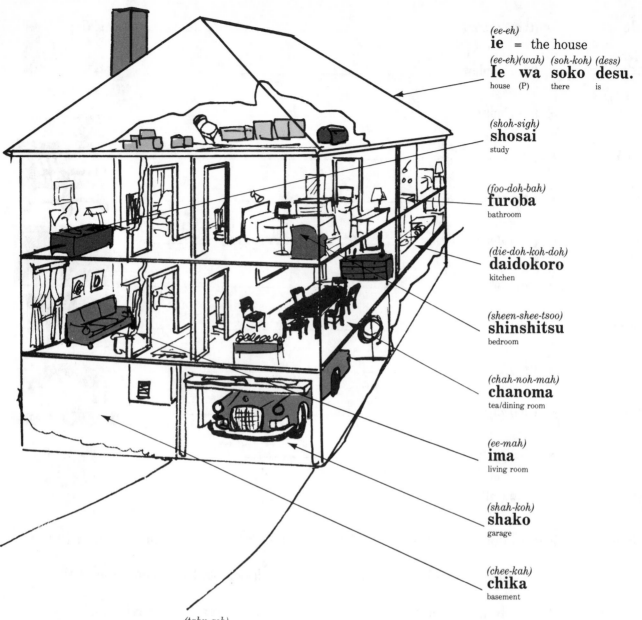

(ee-eh)
ie = the house

(ee-eh)(wah) (soh-koh) (dess)
Ie wa soko desu.
house (P)   there   is

(shoh-sigh)
shosai
study

(foo-doh-bah)
furoba
bathroom

(die-doh-koh-doh)
daidokoro
kitchen

(sheen-shee-tsoo)
shinshitsu
bedroom

(chah-noh-mah)
chanoma
tea/dining room

(ee-mah)
ima
living room

(shah-koh)
shako
garage

(chee-kah)
chika
basement

(tahn-goh)
While learning these new **tango,** let's not forget

(jee-dōh-shah)
jidōsha
car

(jee-ten-shah)
jitensha
bicycle

(ee-noo)
inu
dog

inu

☐ **batterii** *(baht-teh-dēē)*	....	battery	
☐ **beddō** *(bed-dōh)*	....	bed	
☐ **bēkon** *(bēh-kohn)*	....	bacon	
☐ **bēsubōru** *(bēh-soo-bōh-doo)*	....	baseball	
☐ **bifuteki** *(bee-foo-teh-kee)*	....	beefsteak	

(neh-koh)
neko
cat

(nee-wah)
niwa
garden

(yōo-bean)
yūbin
mail

niwa

(yōo-bean-bah-koh)
yūbinbako
mailbox

(hah-nah)
hana
flowers

(yoh-bee-deen)
yobirin
doorbell

Peel off the next set of labels and wander through your **ie** *(ee-eh)* learning these **atarashii tango** *(ah-tah-dah-shēē)*.
house   new

Granted, it will be somewhat difficult to label your **inu,** *(ee-noo)* **neko** *(neh-koh)* or **hana,** *(hah-nah)* but use your
dog   cat   flowers

imagination. Again, practice by asking yourself, **"Niwa wa doko desu ka?"** *(nee-wah)* *(dess)* and reply,
garden (P) where is

"Niwa wa soko desu." *(nee-wah)* *(dess)* Now for the following . . .
there   is

. . . wa doko desu ka?

□ **bijinesuman** *(bee-jee-neh-soo-mahn)* . . . . . businessman
□ **biiru** *(bēē-doo)* . . . . beer
□ **bitamin** *(bee-tah-meen)* . . . . vitamin
□ **botan** *(boh-tahn)* . . . . button
□ **burēki** *(boo-dēh-kee)* . . . . brake

9

Step 4

> (ee-chee) (nee) (sahn)
> ## Ichi, Ni, San
> one   two   three

These are the **tango** to a game that **kodomo** play in **Nihon**.
         (koh-doh-moh)   (nee-hohn)
          children   Japan

> (ee-chee) (gah) (sah-shtah) (nee) (sah-shtah) (sah-shtah)
> **Ichi ga sashita, ni ga sashita, san ga sashita,**
> one   (P)   time   two   times   three   times
>
> (shee) (sah-shtah) (goh) (sah-shtah) (doh-koo) (sah-shtah)
> **Shi ga sashita, go ga sashita, roku ga sashita,**
> four   five   six
>
> (shee-chee) (hah-chee)
> **Shichi ga sashita, hachi ga sashita!**
> seven   eight/bee   stings

In many ways, **bangō** are used differently in **Nihongo** than they are in **Eigo**. Unlike
       (bahn-gōh)   (nee-hohn-goh)   (ay-goh)
       numbers   Japanese   English

(ay-goh)   (nee-hohn-goh)
Eigo, in **Nihongo**, days and months are indicated by **bangō**. For example, **ichi gatsu**,
English   Japanese   (bahn-gōh)   (ee-chee)(gah-tsoo)
                                           numbers   first   month

means January in **Nihongo**. When practicing the **bangō** below, notice the similarities
           (nee-hohn-goh)   (bahn-gōh)
           Japanese   numbers

between **shi** (4) and **jūshi** (14), **shichi** (7) and **jūshichi** (17) and so on. After practicing the
       (shee)   (jōō-shee)   (shee-chee)   (jōō-shee-chee)

bangō out loud, cover the **Nihongo** and write out the **bangō** 1 through 10 below.
(bahn-gōh)   (nee-hohn-goh)   (bahn-gōh)
numbers

0	(zeh-doh) **zero**			0 *zero, zero, zero*
1	(ee-chee) **ichi**	11	(jōō-ee-chee) **jūichi**	1 _____
2	(nee) **ni**	12	(jōō-nee) **jūni**	2 _____
3	(sahn) **san**	13	(jōō-sahn) **jūsan**	3 _____
4	(shee) (yohn) **shi / yon**	14	(jōō-shee) (jōō-yohn) **jūshi / jūyon**	4 _____
5	(goh) **go**	15	(jōō-goh) **jūgo**	5 _____
6	(doh-koo) **roku**	16	(jōō-doh-koo) **jūroku**	6 _____
7	(shee-chee) (nah-nah) **shichi / nana**	17	(jōō-shee-chee) (jōō-nah-nah) **jūshichi / jūnana**	7 _____
8	(hah-chee) **hachi**	18	(jōō-hah-chee) **jūhachi**	8 _____
9	(koo) (kyōō) **ku / kyū**	19	(jōō-koo) (jōō-kyōō) **jūku / jūkyū**	9 _____
10	(jōō) **jū**	20	(nee-jōō) **nijū**	10 _____

☐ **chaneru** (chah-neh-doo) . . . . channel
☐ **chekku** (chek-koo) . . . . check
☐ **chesu** (cheh-soo) . . . . chess
☐ **chippu** (cheep-poo) . . . . tip, gratuity
☐ **chiizu** (chēē-zoo) . . . . cheese

Use these **bangō** *(bahn-goh)* on a daily basis. Practice **bangō** when you brush your teeth, exercise or commute to work. **Bangō** change slightly depending on what they refer to. You will see this in the exercise below. Now fill in the following blanks according to the **bangō** given in parentheses.

numbers

Note: This is a good time to start learning the following important **tango.**

---

kudasai *(koo-dah-sigh)* = please give me _____

Kami *(kah-mee)* o *(oh)* _____ (15) paper (P)	**mai kudasai.** *(my) (koo-dah-sigh)* sheets please give me		**Nan mai?** *(nahn) (my)* _____ (15) how many (M)	
Hagaki *(hah-gah-kee)* o *(oh)* _____ (10) postcards (P)	**mai kudasai.** (M)		**Nan mai?** (M) _____ (10)	
Kitte *(keet-teh)* o *(oh)* _____ (11) stamps (P)	**mai kudasai.** (M)		**Nan mai?** (M) _____ (11)	
Gasorin *(gah-soh-deen)* o _____ (8) gasoline (P)	**rittoru kudasai.** *(deet-toh-doo)* liters		**Nan rittoru?** *(deet-toh-doo)* _____ (8) (M)	
Orenji jūsu *(oh-den-jee) (jōō-soo)* o _____ (3) orange juice (P)	**bai kudasai.** *(by)* glasses		**Nan bai?** *(by)* _____ (3) (M)	
Ocha *(oh-chah)* o _____ (3) tea (P)	**bai kudasai.** *(by)* glasses		**Nan bai?** (M) _____ (3)	
Biiru *(bēē-doo)* o *san* bai kudasai. (3) beer (P)	**bai kudasai.** *(by)*		**Nan bai?** (M) _____ (3)	
Tamago *(tah-mah-goh)* o _____ (12) eggs (P)	**ko kudasai.** *(koh)* (M)		**Nan ko?** *(koh)* _____ (12) (M)	
Kippu *(keep-poo)* o _____ (5) tickets (P)	**mai kudasai.** *(my)* (M)		**Nan mai?** *(my)* _____ (5) (M)	
Mizu *(mee-zoo)* o _____ (3) water (P)	**bai kudasai.** *(by)* glasses		**Nan bai?** *(by)* _____ (3) (M)	
Budōshu *(boo-dōh-shoo)* o _____ (3) wine (P)	**bai kudasai.** (M)		**Nan bai?** (M) _____ (3)	
E *(eh)* o _____ (6) pictures (P)	**mai kudasai.** *(my)* (M)		**Nan mai?** *(my)* *roku* (6) (M)	

- ☐ **daiyamondo** *(die-yah-mohn-doh)* . . . . diamond _____
- ☐ **dekorēshon** *(deh-koh-dēh-shohn)* . . . . decoration _____
- ☐ **demo** *(deh-moh)* . . . . demonstration _____
- ☐ **depāto** *(deh-pāh-toh)* . . . . department store _____
- ☐ **dezain** *(deh-zine)* . . . . design _____

Now see if you can translate the following thoughts into **Nihongo.** *(nee-hohn-goh)* **Kotae** *(koh-tah-eh)* are at the answers

bottom of the **pēji.** *(pēh-jee)* page Give it your best.

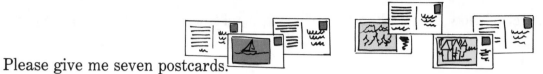

1. Please give me seven postcards.

_____

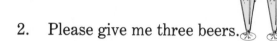

2. Please give me three beers. _____

3. Please give me three glasses of water.

_____

4. Please give me five tickets.

Kippu o go mai kudasai.

Now, review the **bangō** *(bahn-gōh)* numbers 1 through 20, answer the following **shitsumon** *(shee-tsoo-mohn)* questions aloud, and then
write out the **kotae.** *(koh-tah-eh)* answers Notice how **arimasu** *(ah-dee-mahss)* is/are and **ikutsu** *(ee-koo-tsoo)* how many are used with inanimate objects and
imasu *(ee-mahss)* is/are and **nannin** *(nahn-neen)* how many are used with people.

Koko ni tēburu ga *(koh-koh) (nee) (tēh-boo-doo) (gah)*
here (P) tables
ikutsu arimasu ka? *(ee-koo-tsoo) (ah-dee-mahss)*
how many are there?

san

Koko ni ranpu ga
here lamps *(dahn-poo)*
ikutsu arimasu ka? *(ee-koo-tsoo) (ah-dee-mahss)*
how many are there?

_____

Koko ni isu ga
here chairs *(ee-soo)*
ikutsu arimasu ka? *(ee-koo-tsoo) (ah-dee-mahss)*
how many are there?

_____

KOTAE

1. **Hagaki o nana mai kudasai.**   2. **Biiru o san bai kudasai.**

3. **Mizu o san bai kudasai.**   4. **Kippu o go mai kudasai.**

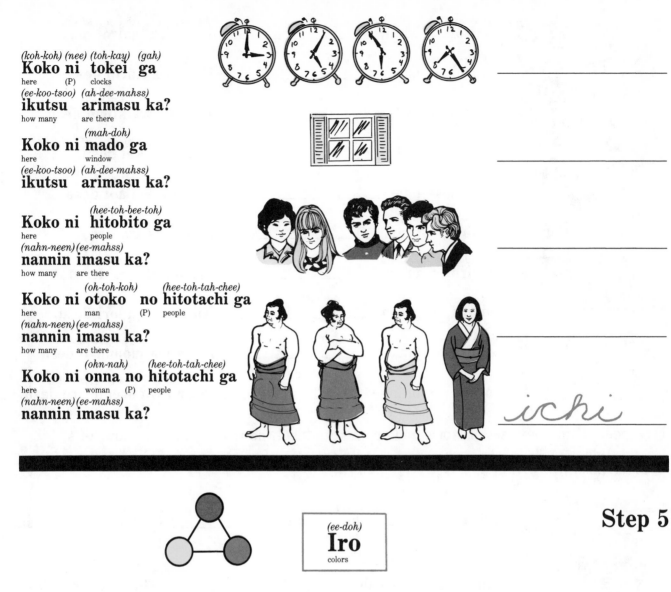

(koh-koh) (nee) (toh-kay) (gah)
Koko ni tokei ga
here (P) clocks
(ee-koo-tsoo) (ah-dee-mahss)
ikutsu arimasu ka?
how many are there

Koko ni mado ga *(mah-doh)*
here window
(ee-koo-tsoo) (ah-dee-mahss)
ikutsu arimasu ka?

Koko ni hitobito ga *(hee-toh-bee-toh)*
here people
(nahn-neen) (ee-mahss)
nannin imasu ka?
how many are there

(oh-toh-koh) (hee-toh-tah-chee)
Koko ni otoko no hitotachi ga
here man (P) people
(nahn-neen) (ee-mahss)
nannin imasu ka?
how many are there

(ohn-nah) (hee-toh-tah-chee)
Koko ni onna no hitotachi ga
here woman (P) people
(nahn-neen) (ee-mahss)
nannin imasu ka?

ichi

(ee-doh)
Iro
colors

Step 5

(ee-doh) *(nee-hohn)* *(ah-meh-dee-kah)* *(nah-mah-eh)*
Iro are the same in **Nihon** as they are in **Amerika** — they just have different **namae.** You
colors America names

should be able to learn them quickly. For instance, you should be able to easily recognize

(oh-den-jee) *(toh-moh-dah-chee)*
"**orenji**" as "orange." Note that if you ever have to visit a **tomodachi** in the hospital, you
friend

(hah-nah) *(ah-kye)* *(tah-shoh-koo)* *(hah-nah)* *(shee-doy)* *(kee-doy)*
should take **hana** that are **akai** or **tashoku.** Do not take **hana** that are **shiroi** or **kiiroi** —
flowers red multicolored flowers white yellow

(ee-doh)
they are for mourning. Now let's learn the basic **iro.** Once you have read through the list
colors

(peh-jee) *(teh)*
on the next **pēji,** cover the **Nihongo** with your **te,** and practice writing out the **Nihongo**
hand

(ay-goh)
next to the **Eigo.**
English

☐ **direkutā** *(dee-deh-koo-tāh)* .... director
☐ **dezāto** *(deh-zāh-toh)* .... dessert
☐ **dorai kuriiningu** *(doh-die) (koo-dēē-neen-goo)* . dry cleaning
☐ **dorama** *(doh-dah-mah)* .... drama
☐ **doru** *(doh-doo)* .... dollar

13

(shee-doy)
shiroi = white _____
(foo-neh) (wah) (shee-doy) (dess)
Fune wa shiroi desu.
boat   is

(koo-doy)
kuroi = black _____
(bōh-doo) (koo-doy)
Bōru wa kuroi desu.
ball

(kēē-doy)
kiiroi = yellow _____
(bah-nah-nah) (kēē-doy)
Banana wa kiiroi desu.
banana

(ah-kye)
akai = red _akai_
(hohn) (ah-kye)
Hon wa akai desu.
book

(ah-oy)
aoi = blue _____
(jee-dōh-shah) (ah-oy)
Jidōsha wa aoi desu.
car

(hi-doh)
haiiro = gray _____
(zōh) (hi-doh)
Zō wa haiiro desu.
elephant

(chi-doh)
chairo = brown _____
(ee-soo) (chi-doh)
Isu wa chairo desu.
chair

(mee-doh-dee)
midori = green _____
(koo-sah) (mee-doh-dee)
Kusa wa midori desu.
grass

(moh-moh-ee-doh)
momoiro = pink _____
(hah-nah) (moh-moh-ee-doh)
Hana wa momoiro desu.
flower

(oh-den-jee)
orenji = orange _____
(dahn-poo) (oh-den-jee) (ee-doh)
Ranpu wa orenji iro desu.
lamp   orange   color

Now peel off the next set of labels and proceed to label the **iro** in your **ie.** Now let's
(ee-doh) colors *(ee-eh)* house

practice using these **tango.**
(tahn-goh) words

(shee-doy) (foo-neh) (wah) (doh-koh) (dess) (kah)
Shiroi fune wa doko desu ka? _____
white boat (P) where is
(foo-neh)(wah) (soh-koh) (dess)
fune wa soko desu.
(P) there is

(koo-doy) (tēh-boo-doo)
Kuroi tēburu wa doko desu ka? _____
black table
(tēh-boo-doo)
tēburu wa soko desu.

(chi-doh) (ee-soo)
Chairo no isu wa doko desu ka? _____
brown (P) chair
(ee-soo)
no isu wa soko desu.
(P)

Shiroi bōru wa doko desu ka? _____
(bōh-doo)
ball
(bōh-doo)
bōru wa soko desu.

(ah-oy) (dahn-poo)
Aoi ranpu wa doko desu ka? _aoi_
blue
(dahn-poo)
ranpu wa soko desu.

(ah-kye) (hohn)
Akai hon wa doko desu ka? _____
red book
(hohn)
hon wa soko desu.

(moh-moh-ee-doh) *(ee-eh)*
Momoiro no ie wa doko desu ka? _____ *(ee-eh)* **no ie wa soko desu.**
pink   (P) house   (P)

(hi-doh) *(doh-ah)* *(doh-koh)* *(dess)*
Haiiro no doa wa doko desu ka? _____ *(doh-ah)* *(soh-koh)* *(dess)* **no doa wa soko desu.**
gray   (P) door (P) where is   (P)   (P) there is

(kēē-doy) *(bah-nah-nah)*
Kiiroi banana wa doko desu ka? _____ *(bah-nah-nah)* **banana wa soko desu.**
yellow   banana

Note: In **Nihongo,** the verb for "have" is **motte imasu.** *(moht-teh)* *(ee-mahss)*

(moht-teh) *(ee-mahss)*
motte imasu **=**

I have _____

we have _____

Let's review *(koo-dah-sigh)* **kudasai** and learn *(moht-teh)* *(ee-mahss)* **motte imasu.** Repeat each sentence out loud.

(bēē-doo) *(sahn) (by)* *(koo-dah-sigh)*
Biiru o san bai kudasai.
beer (P) three glasses please give me

(boo-dōh-shoo) *(nee) (hi)*
Budōshu o ni hai kudasai.
wine   two glasses

(sah-dah-dah)
Sarada o kudasai.
salad

(jee-dōh-shah)
Jidōsha o kudasai.
car

(hah-gah-kee)
Hagaki o kudasai.
postcard

(bēē-doo) *(sahn) (by)* *(moht-teh)* *(ee-mahss)*
Biiru o san bai motte imasu.
          three glasses I have

(boo-dōh-shoo) *(nee) (hi)* *(moht-teh)* *(ee-mahss)*
Budōshu o ni hai motte imasu.
wine   two glasses we have

(sah-dah-dah)
Sarada o motte imasu.
salad

(jee-dōh-shah)
Jidōsha o motte imasu.
car

(hah-gah-kee)
Hagaki o motte imasu.
postcard

Now fill in the following blanks with **kudasai** or **motte imasu.**

(jee-dōh-shah) *(sahn) (die)*
Jidōsha o san dai _____*motte imasu*_____.
cars   three   (we have)

(keep-poo) *(nee) (my)*
Kippu o ni mai _____.
tickets   two (M)   (please give me)

(eh)
E o _____.
picture   (I have)

(hah-gah-kee) *(nah-nah) (my)*
Hagaki o nana mai _____.
postcards   seven (M)   (please give me)

☐ **enerugī** *(eh-neh-doo-gēē)* .... energy   _____
☐ **enjin** *(en-jeen)* .... engine   _____
☐ **epuron** *(eh-poo-dohn)* .... apron   _____
☐ **erebētā** *(eh-deh-bēh-tāh)* .... elevator   _____
☐ **esukarētā** *(eh-skah-dēh-tāh)* .... escalator   _____

15

(koh-koh) (nee)
Koko ni a quick review of **iro.** Draw lines between the **Nihongo no** **tango** and the correct
here   is   colors   Japanese (P)   words
(ee-doh)
iro. On your mark, get set, *GO!*
colors

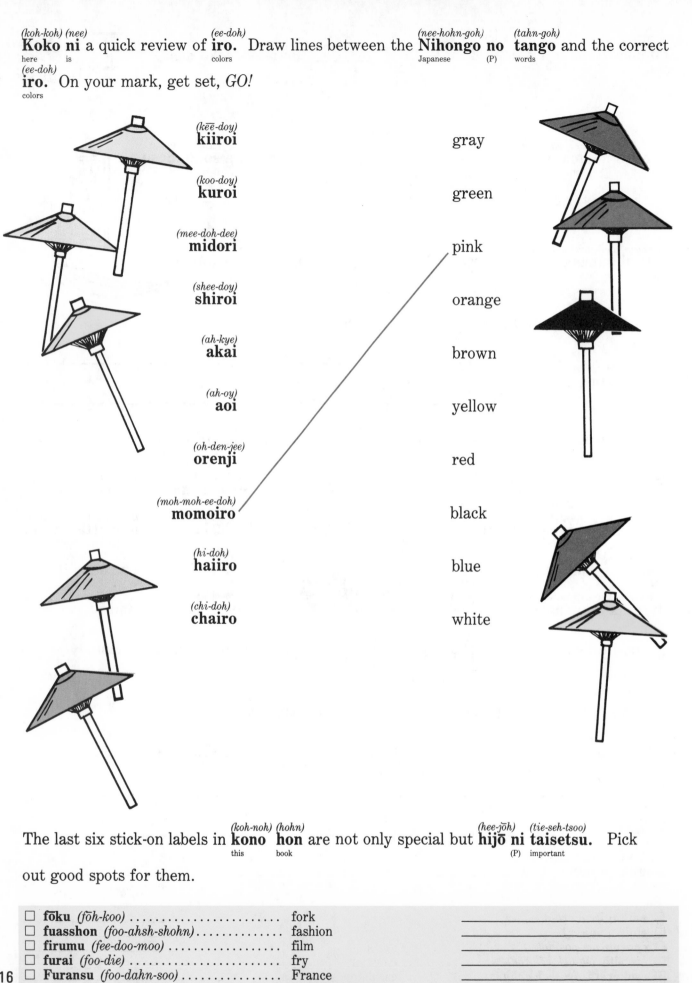

(kee-doy)
kiiroi   gray

(koo-doy)
kuroi   green

(mee-doh-dee)
midori   pink

(shee-doy)
shiroi   orange

(ah-kye)
akai   brown

(ah-oy)
aoi   yellow

(oh-den-jee)
orenji   red

(moh-moh-ee-doh)
momoiro   black

(hi-doh)
haiiro   blue

(chi-doh)
chairo   white

(koh-noh) (hohn)   **(hee-jōh) (tie-seh-tsoo)**
The last six stick-on labels in **kono** **hon** are not only special but **hijō ni taisetsu.** Pick
this   book   (P)   important

out good spots for them.

☐ **fōku** *(fōh-koo)* .... fork   _____
☐ **fuasshon** *(foo-ahsh-shohn)* .... fashion   _____
☐ **firumu** *(fee-doo-moo)* .... film   _____
☐ **furai** *(foo-die)* .... fry   _____
16 ☐ **Furansu** *(foo-dahn-soo)* .... France   _____

(oh-kah-neh)
Okane
money

Before starting this Step, go back and review Step 4. Make sure you can count to **nijū** *(nee-jōō)* 20

without looking at **kono** *(koh-noh)* **hon.** *(hohn)* Let's learn the larger **bangō** *(bahn-gōh)* now, so if something costs
this   book   numbers

more than 20 **en,** *(en)* you will know exactly **ikura** *(ee-koo-dah)* it costs. After practicing aloud the
yen   how much

Nihongo *(nee-hohn-goh)* **no** **bangō** *(bahn-gōh)* 10 through 5000 below, write these **bangō** *(bahn-gōh)* in the blanks provided.
Japanese   (P)   numbers

Again, notice the similarities between **bangō** such as **roku** *(doh-koo)* (6), **jūroku** *(jōō-doh-koo)* (16), and **rokujū** *(doh-koo-jōō)* (60).

10	**jū** *(jōō)*	(**yon** *(yohn)* + **roku** *(doh-koo)* = **jū**) *(jōō)*			**10** ~~jū, jū, jū, jū~~
20	**nijū** *(nee-jōō)*	(**ni** *(nee)* = 2)			**20** _____
30	**sanjū** *(sahn-jōō)*	(**san** *(sahn)* = 3)			**30** _____
40	**yonjū** *(yohn-jōō)*	(**yon** *(yohn)* = 4)			**40** _____
50	**gojū** *(goh-jōō)*	(**go** *(goh)* = 5)			**50** _____
60	**rokujū** *(doh-koo-jōō)*	(**roku** *(doh-koo)* = 6)			**60** _____
70	**nanajū** *(nah-nah-jōō)*	(**nana** *(nah-nah)* = 7)			**70** _____
80	**hachijū** *(hah-chee-jōō)*	(**hachi** *(hah-chee)* = 8)			**80** _____
90	**kyūjū** *(kyōō-jōō)*	(**kyū** *(kyōō)* = 9)			**90** _____
100	**hyaku** *(hyah-koo)*				**100** _____
500	**gohyaku** *(goh-hyah-koo)*				**500** _____
1000	**sen** *(sen)*				**1000** _____
5000	**gosen** *(goh-sen)*				**5000** _____

Now take a logical guess. How would you write (and say) the following? **Kotae** are at

the bottom of **kono** *(koh-noh)* **pēji.** *(pēh-jee)*
this   page

400 _____   700 _____

2000 _____   5500 _____

The unit of currency in **Nihon** *(nee-hohn)* [Japan] is the **en,** *(en)* [yen] abbreviated **¥**. Bills are called **satsu** *(sah-tsoo)* and coins are called **kōka.** *(kōh-kah)* Whereas an American **doru** *(doh-doo)* [dollar] can be broken down into 100 pennies, a 500 **en satsu** *(en) (sah-tsoo)* [yen bill] can be divided into 500 **ichi en kōka.** *(ee-chee) (en) (kōh-kah)* [one yen coins] (You will also hear **dama** *(dah-mah)* used in place of **kōka.**) Let's learn the various kinds of **satsu to kōka.** *(sah-tsoo) (toh) (kōh-kah)* [and] Always be sure to practice each **tango** out loud. You might want to exchange some money now so that you can familiarize yourself with the various **satsu to kōka.** [and]

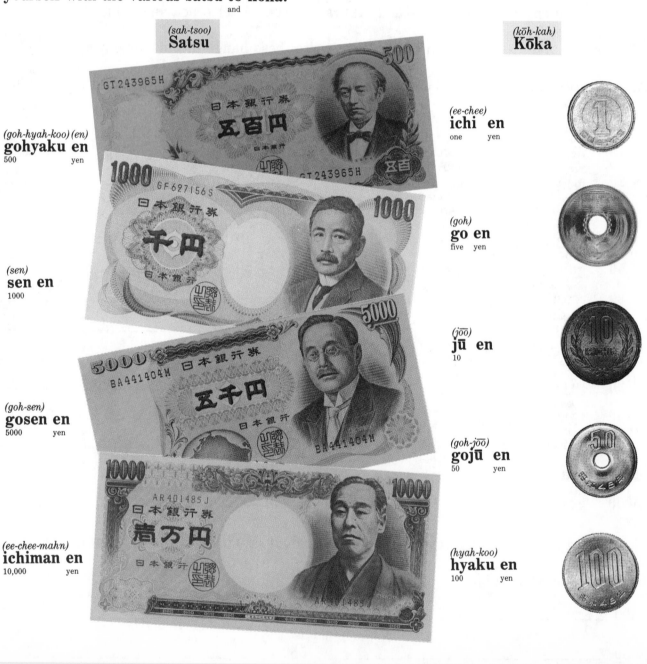

Satsu *(sah-tsoo)*

gohyaku en *(goh-hyah-koo) (en)*
500 yen

sen en *(sen)*
1000

gosen en *(goh-sen)*
5000 yen

ichiman en *(ee-chee-mahn)*
10,000 yen

Kōka *(kōh-kah)*

ichi en *(ee-chee)*
one yen

go en *(goh)*
five yen

jū en *(jōō)*
10

gojū en *(goh-jōō)*
50 yen

hyaku en *(hyah-koo)*
100 yen

☐ **furiiza** *(foo-dēē-zah)* . . . . freezer _____
☐ **furūtsu** *(foo-dōō-tsoo)* . . . . fruit _____
  — **furūtsu jūsu** *(foo-dōō-tsoo) (jōō-soo)* . . . . fruit juice _____
  — **furūtsu sarada** *(foo-dōō-tsoo) (sah-dah-dah)* . . fruit salad _____
☐ **futtobōru** *(foot-toh-bōh-doo)* . . . . football

Review the **bangō jū** *(bahn-gōh) (jōō)* through **gosen** *(goh-sen)*. Now, how do you say "twenty-two" or "fifty-three"
numbers 10 · 5000

in **Nihongo?** *(nee-hohn-goh)* You actually do a bit of arithmetic: 5 **(go)** *(goh)* times 10 **(jū)** *(jōō)* plus 3 **(san)** *(sahn)* equals 53
Japanese

(gojūsan). *(goh-jōō-sahn)* See if you can say and write out the **bangō** *(bahn-gōh)* on **kono** *(koh-noh)* **pēji.** *(pēh-jee)* **Kotae** are at the
this · page

bottom of the **pēji.**

a. 25 = _____
(2 x 10) + 5

b. 47 = _____
(4 x 10) + 7

c. 84 = _____
(8 x 10) + 4

d. 51 = *gojūichi*
(5 x 10) + 1

e. 36 = _____
(3 x 10) + 6

f. 93 = _____
(9 x 10) + 3

g. 68 = _____
(6 x 10) + 8

h. 72 = _____
(7 x 10) + 2

To ask how much something costs in **Nihongo,** *(nee-hohn-goh)* one asks, **"Ikura desu ka?"** *(ee-koo-dah) (dess) (kah)* **Ima** *(ee-mah)* answer
how much · is it · now

the following questions based on the **bangō** *(bahn-gōh)* in parentheses.
numbers

1. **Kore wa ikura desu ka?** *(koh-deh)(wah) (ee-koo-dah) (dess) (kah)*
this (P) how much is
_____ **en desu.** *(en) (dess)*
(10) · yen

2. **Sore wa ikura desu ka?** *(soh-deh) (ee-koo-dah) (dess)*
that (P) how much is
_____ **en desu.**
(20)

3. **Hon wa ikura desu ka?** *(hohn)*
book
_____ **en desu.**
(250)

4. **Hagaki wa ikura desu ka?** *(hah-gah-kee)*
postcard
Hachijū **en desu.**
(80)

5. **Firumu wa ikura desu ka?** *(fee-doo-moo)*
film
_____ **en desu.**
(750)

6. **Heya no dai wa ikura desu ka?** *(heh-yah) (die)*
room (P) rent
_____ **en desu.**
(4000)

7. **E wa ikura desu ka?** *(eh)*
picture
_____ **en desu.**
(2000)

KOTAE		
		Congratulations!
e. **sanjūroku**	2. **nijū**	7. **nisen**
d. **gojūichi**	1. **jū**	6. **yonsen**
c. **hachijūyon**	h. **nanajūni**	5. **nanahyakugojū**
b. **yonjūnana**	g. **rokujūhachi**	4. **hachijū**
a. **nijūgo**	f. **kyūjūsan**	3. **nihyakugojū**

19

Step 7

(kyōh) today	*(ah-shtah)* tomorrow	*(kee-nōh)* yesterday

Kyō, Ashita, Kinō

(kah-den-dāh)
Karendā
calendar

(eesh-shōō-kahn)   *(nah-noh-kah-kahn)*
Isshūkan wa nanokakan desu.
one week   (P)   seven days   has

(geh-tsoo-yōh-bee) **Getsuyōbi**	*(kah-yōh-bee)* **Kayōbi**	*(soo-ee-yōh-bee)* **Suiyōbi**	*(moh-koo-yōh-bee)* **Mokuyōbi**	*(keen-yōh-bee)* **Kinyōbi**	*(doh-yōh-bee)* **Doyōbi**	*(nee-chee-yōh-bee)* **Nichiyōbi**
1	2	3	4	5	6	7

(hee-jōh)(nee) (tie-seh-tsoo)

It is **hijō ni taisetsu** to know the days of the week and the various parts of the day.
very   (P)   important

Let's learn them. Be sure to say them aloud before filling in the blanks below. Note that

the Japanese begin counting their week on Monday with *(geh-tsoo-yōh-bee)* **Getsuyōbi.**

(geh-tsoo-yōh-bee)
Getsuyōbi _____
Monday

(kah-yōh-bee)
Kayōbi _____
Tuesday

(soo-ee-yōh-bee)
Suiyōbi _____
Wednesday

(moh-koo-yōh-bee)
Mokuyōbi _____
Thursday

(keen-yōh-bee)
Kinyōbi _____
Friday

(doh-yōh-bee)
Doyōbi *Doyōbi*
Saturday

(nee-chee-yōh-bee)
Nichiyōbi _____
Sunday

(kyōh)   *(soo-ee-yōh-bee)* *(dess)*   *(ah-shtah)*   *(moh-koo-yōh-bee)*   *(kee-nōh)* *(kah-yōh-bee)* *(deh-shtah)*

If **kyō wa Suiyōbi desu,** then **ashita wa Mokuyōbi desu** and **kinō wa Kayōbi deshita.**
today (P) Wednesday is   tomorrow (P) Thursday   is   yesterday (P) Tuesday   was

Now, you supply the correct answers. If **kyō wa Getsuyōbi desu,** then **ashita wa**
(kyōh) *(geh-tsoo-yōh-bee)* *(ah-shtah)*
today (P) Monday   tomorrow (P)

_____ **desu** and **kinō wa** _____ **deshita.** Or, if **kyō wa Getsuyōbi**
(kee-nōh) *(deh-shtah)* *(kyōh)* *(geh-tsoo-yōh-bee)*
yesterday (P)   was   today (P) Monday

desu, then *ashita* **wa Kayōbi desu** and _____ **wa Nichiyōbi deshita.**
(kah-yōh-bee) *(nee-chee-yōh-bee)* *(deh-shtah)*
Tuesday   (P) Sunday   was

Kyō wa nan yōbi desu ka? Kyō wa _____ **desu.**
(nahn)(yōh-bee)
today (P) what day of the week is

(ee-mah)   *(nah-nah)(my)*   *(kah-den-dāh)*

Ima, peel off the next **nana mai** labels and put them on a **karendā** that you use every day.
now   seven (M)   calendar

(geh-tsoo-yōh-bee)
From now on, Monday is "**Getsuyōbi.**"

☐ **gaido** *(guy-doh)*	guide	_____
☐ **garēji** *(gah-dēh-jee)*	garage	_____
☐ **gasorin** *(gah-soh-deen)*	gasoline	_____
☐ **gāze** *(gāh-zeh)*	gauze	_____
☐ **gēmu** *(gēh-moo)*	game	_____

20

There are **yon** *(yohn)* **bun** *(boon)* to each **hi** *(hee)*.
four   parts   day

morning =	**asa** *(ah-sah)*	*asa, asa, asa, asa*
afternoon =	**gogo** *(goh-goh)*	_____
evening =	**ban** *(bahn)*	_____
night =	**yoru** *(yoh-doo)*	_____

Also, in **Nihongo, hiruma** *(nee-hohn-goh) (hee-doo-mah)* means "daytime" or "midday" and **kesa** *(keh-sah)* means "this morning."

Now, fill in the following blanks and then check your answers at the bottom of **kono** *(koh-noh)* **pēji** *(pēh-jee)*.
this   page

Always add **"no"** between the **hi** *(hee)* and the part of the day.
day

a. Sunday morning = _____

b. Friday evening = *Kinyōbi no ban*

c. Saturday evening = _____

d. Monday morning = _____

e. Wednesday morning = _____

f. Tuesday afternoon = _____

g. Thursday afternoon = _____

h. Thursday night = _____

i. yesterday evening = _____

j. yesterday afternoon = _____

k. yesterday morning = *kinō no asa*

l. tomorrow morning = _____

m. tomorrow afternoon = _____

n. tomorrow evening = _____

o. tomorrow night = _____

KOTAE

o. **ashita no yoru**	j. **kinō no gogo**	e. **Suiyōbi no asa**
n. **ashita no ban**	i. **kinō no ban**	d. **Getsuyōbi no asa**
m. **ashita no gogo**	h. **Mokuyōbi no yoru**	c. **Doyōbi no ban**
l. **ashita no asa**	g. **Mokuyōbi no gogo**	b. **Kinyōbi no ban**
k. **kinō no asa**	f. **Kayōbi no gogo**	a. **Nichiyōbi no asa**

21

So, with merely **jūichi no tango**, you can specify any **hi** of the **shūkan** and any time of
(jōō-ee-chee) *(tahn-goh)* *(hee)* *(shōō-kahn)*
eleven (P) words day week

the **hi**. The words **kyō**, **ashita** and **kinō** will be **hijō ni taisetsu** for you in making
(hee) *(kyōh)* *(ah-shtah)* *(kee-nōh)* *(hee-jōh)(nee) (tie-seh-tsoo)*
today tomorrow yesterday very (P) important

reservations **to** appointments, in getting **kippu** for a **geki** or **eiga** and for many other
(keep-poo) *(geh-kee)* *(ay-gah)*
and tickets play movie

things you will wish to do. Knowing the parts of the **hi** will help you to learn and
(hee)
day

understand the various **Nihongo** greetings below. Practice these every day until your trip.

good morning =	**ohayō gozaimasu** *(oh-hi-yōh) (goh-zye-mahss)*
good night =	**oyasuminasai** *(oh-yah-soo-mee-nah-sigh)*
good day/hello =	**konnichi wa** *(kohn-nee-chee)(wah)*
good evening =	**konban wa** *(kohn-bahn)*
How are you? =	**Ogenki desu ka?** *(oh-gen-kee)*

konnichi wa

Take the next **yon mai** labels and stick them on the appropriate **mono** in your **ie**. How
(yohn) *(moh-noh)* *(ee-eh)*
four (M) things house

about the bathroom mirror for "**ohayō gozaimasu**"? Or your kitchen cabinet for
(oh-hi-yōh) (goh-zye-mahss)

"**konnichi wa**"? Or your alarm clock for "**oyasuminasai**" or the front door for **konban**
(kohn-nee-chee) *(oh-yah-soo-mee-nah-sigh)* *(kohn-bahn)*

wa? Remember that, whenever you enter small shops **to** stores in **Nihon,** you will hear the
(toh) *(nee-hohn)*
and

appropriate greeting for the time of day. It is a **hijō ni** friendly and warm custom.
(hee-jōh)(nee)
very (P)

Everyone greets everyone and you should too, if you really want to enjoy **Nihon!**

You are about one-fourth of your way through **kono hon** and it is a good time to quickly
(hohn)
this book

review the **tango** you have learned before doing the **kurossuwādo** on the next **pēji**.
(tahn-goh) *(koo-dohs-soo-wāh-doh)* *(pēh-jee)*
words crossword puzzle page

Tanoshinde kudasai.
(tah-noh-sheen-deh)
have fun

KUROSSUWĀDO NO KOTAE

ACROSS		DOWN	
2. asa	27. basu	1. bangō	25. ashita
4. shako	28. satsu	3. Mokuyōbi	22. hagaki
6. hoteru	32. shinshitsu	4. shichi	20. takushii
8. kyō	34. resutoran	5. kotae	19. ie
10. kiiroi	36. ban	7. tokei	18. isu
12. kinō	39. jidōsha	9. yoru	16. roku
13. budōshu	40. tegami	11. kippu	14. sarada
15. biiru	42. okane	12. katen	12. katen
17. oyasuminasai	45. pen	14. sarada	11. kippu
21. Nihongo	47. niju	16. roku	9. yoru
23. densha	48. neko	18. isu	7. tokei
24. kado	49. hairiro	19. ie	5. kotae
26. mado		20. takushii	4. shichi
		22. hagaki	3. Mokuyōbi
		25. ashita	1. bangō
			29. niwa
			30. furoba
			31. ginkō
			32. san
			33. Nichiyōbi
			35. doa
			36. bata
			37. denwa
			38. kitte
			39. jūshichi
			41. banana
			43. kuroi
			44. fune
			46. aoi
			47. nan

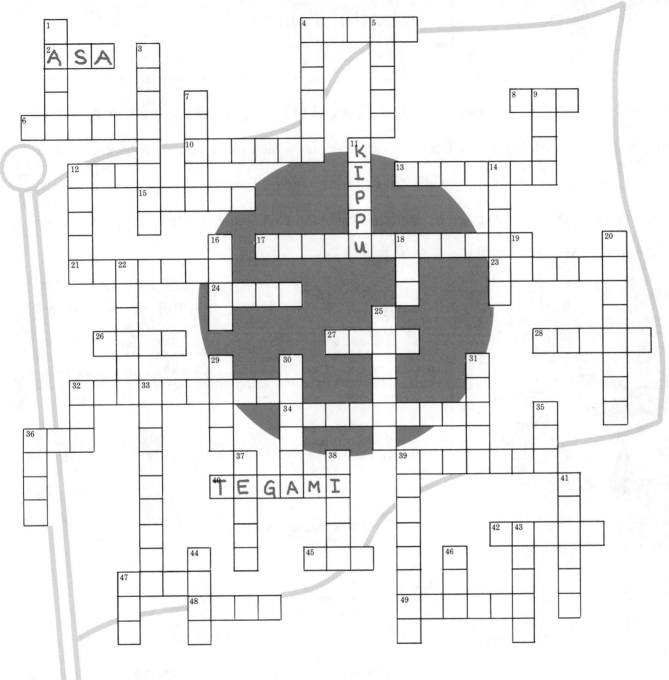

ACROSS

2. morning
4. garage
6. hotel
8. today
10. yellow
12. yesterday
13. wine
15. beer
17. good night
21. Japanese (language)
23. train
24. corner
26. window
27. bus
28. bill/currency
32. bedroom
34. restaurant
36. evening
39. car
40. letter
42. money
45. pen
47. twenty
48. cat
49. gray

DOWN

1. number
3. Thursday
4. seven
5. answers
7. clock
9. night
11. tickets
12. curtain
14. salad
16. six
18. chair
19. house
20. taxi
22. post cards
25. tomorrow
29. garden
30. bathroom
31. bank
32. three
33. Sunday
35. door
36. butter
37. telephone
38. stamps
39. seventeen
41. banana
43. black
44. boat
46. blue
47. what

23

Step 8

(oo-eh) *(shtah)* *(toh-nah-dee)*
Ue, Shita, Tonari
over   under   next to

While in **Nihon,** *(nee-hohn)* prepositions (words like "in," "on," and "next to") will allow you to be precise with a minimum amount of effort. Instead of having to point **roku** *(doh-koo)* times at a piece of jewelry you wish to buy, you can explain precisely which piece you want by saying it is behind, next to, or under the jewelry that the salesperson is starting to pick up. Let's learn some of these little **tango** by studying the examples below. Note that prepositions in **Nihongo** follow the noun and are preceded by **no.**

(kah-dah) **kara** = from	*(P)* *(toh-nah-dee)* **tonari** = next to	*(shtah)* **shita** = under/below
(nee) **ni** = in/into/at		*(oo-eh)* **ue** = over/above

(ah-noh) (oh-toh-koh) (hee-toh) (ah-tah-dah-shee)(hoh-teh-doo)(nee) (hi-dee-mahss)
Ano otoko no hito wa atarashii hoteru ni hairimasu.
that   man   (P)   person   new   hotel   into   enters

(ohn-nah) (hee-toh) (ah-tah-dah-shee) (kah-dah)(deh-mahss)
Ano onna no hito wa atarashii na hoteru kara demasu.
   woman   (P)   person   (P)   (P)   from   leaves

(ee-shah) (ee) (nee) (ee-mahss)
Ano isha wa ii hoteru ni imasu.
   doctor   (P)   good   in   is

(ah-tah-dah-shee) (eh) (teh-boo-doo) (oo-eh)
Atarashii e wa tēburu no ue desu.
new   picture (P)   table   (P)   over   is
(ah-oy) (toh-kay) (toh-nah-dee)
Atarashii e wa aoi tokei no tonari desu.
           blue   clock   (P)   next to
(hi-doh) (ee-noo) (chi-doh) (shtah) (ee-mahss)
Ano haiiro no inu wa chairo no tēburu no shita ni imasu.
     gray   (P)   dog   (P)   (P)   under   (P)   is
(chi-doh)   *(hi-doh)*   *(oo-eh)*
Chairo no tēburu wa haiiro no inu no ue desu.
brown   (P)   gray   (P)   over
(ah-oy)   *(oo-eh)*
Aoi tokei wa tēburu no ue desu.
blue   (P)   (P)   over   is
(eh)   *(toh-nah-dee)*
Aoi tokei wa e no tonari desu.
         (P)   picture (P)   next to

☐ **gomu** *(goh-moo)*	rubber, gum	_____
☐ **gorufu** *(goh-doo-foo)*	golf	_____
☐ **guramu** *(goo-dah-moo)*	gram	_____
☐ **gurasu** *(goo-dah-soo)*	glass	_____
☐ **gurūpu** *(goo-dōō-poo)*	group	_____

Fill in the blanks below with the correct prepositions according to the **e** *(eh)* on the

picture

previous **pēji.** *(pēh-jee)*

page

Ano otoko no hito wa hoteru _____ hairimasu. *(ah-noh) (oh-toh-koh) (hee-toh) (hoh-teh-doo)* *(hi-dee-mahss)*

that man (P) person (P)   enters

Tokei wa e no _____ desu. *(toh-kay) (eh)*

clock   picture (P)

Ano e wa tēburu no *ue* _____ desu. *(eh) (tēh-boo-doo)*

picture table   (P)

Tokei wa tēburu no _____ desu. *(tēh-boo-doo)*

table   (P)

Ano onna no hito wa hoteru _____ demasu. *(ah-noh) (ohn-nah) (hee-toh)* *(deh-mahss)*

that woman (P) person   leaves

Ano isha wa hoteru _____ imasu. *(ee-shah)*

doctor   is

Ano inu wa tēburu no _____ ni imasu. *(ee-noo)* *(ee-mahss)*

dog   (P)   (P) is

Tēburu wa e no _____ desu. *(eh)*

(P)

Chairo no tēburu wa inu no _____ desu. *(chi-doh)* *(ee-noo)*

brown   dog (P)

E wa tokei no _____ desu. *(eh)*

picture   (P)

Now, answer these questions based on the **e** *(eh)* on the previous **pēji.**

picture

Isha wa doko ni imasu ka? _____ *(ee-shah) (doh-koh) (ee-mahss)*

doctor where (P) is

Inu wa doko ni imasu ka? _____ *(ee-noo)*

dog (P)   (P)

Tēburu wa doko desu ka? _____ *(tēh-boo-doo)*

table   (P) where is

E wa doko desu ka? *E wa tokei no tonari desu.* *(eh)*

picture

Ano onna no hito wa nani o shite imasu ka? _____ *(ah-noh) (ohn-nah) (hee-toh) (nah-nee) (shtay) (ee-mahss)*

that woman (P) person what (P)   doing

Ano otoko no hito wa nani o shite imasu ka? _____ *(oh-toh-koh) (hee-toh) (nah-nee) (shtay)*

man (P) person what (P)   doing

Tokei wa aoi desu ka? _____ *(toh-kay) (ah-oy)*

clock (P) blue is

Inu wa haiiro desu ka? _____ *(ee-noo) (hi-doh)*

dog gray is

☐ **haikingu** *(hi-keen-goo)*	hiking	_____
☐ **hanbāgu** *(hahn-bāh-goo)*	hamburger	_____
☐ **handobaggu** *(hahn-doh-bahg-goo)*	handbag	_____
☐ **handobōru** *(hahn-doh-bōh-doo)*	handball	_____
☐ **hankache** *(hahn-kah-chee)*	handkerchief	_____

25

Now for some more **renshū** *(den-shōō)* with **Nihongo** *(nee-hohn-goh)* prepositions!
practice   Japanese

aïda *(ay-dah)*	=	between
mae *(my)*	=	in front of
ushiro *(oo-shee-doh)*	=	behind
ni *(nee)*	=	on (Yes, **"ni"** also means "in.")
ue *(oo-eh)*	=	on top (And yes, **"ue"** also means "over" or "above.")

Mizu wa tēburu no ue desu. *(mee-zoo) (tēh-boo-doo) (oo-eh)*
water (P) table (P) on top is

E wa kabe ni kakarimasu. *(eh) (kah-beh) (nee) (kah-kah-dee-mahss)*
picture wall on hangs

Ranpu wa tēburu no ushiro desu. *(dahn-poo) (tēh-boo-doo) (oo-shee-doh)*
lamp table (P) behind

Tēburu wa beddo no mae desu. *(bed-doh) (my)*
bed (P) in front of

Kiiroi ranpu wa tēburu to beddo *(kēē-doy) (dahn-poo) (toh)*
yellow lamp (P) and

no aïda desu. *(ay-dah)*
(P) between

Mizu wa tēburu no *ue* desu.

E wa kabe _____ kakarimasu.

Ranpu wa tēburu no _____ desu.

Tēburu wa beddo no _____ desu.

Kiiroi ranpu wa tēburu to beddo

no _____ desu.

Answer the following **shitsumon,** *(shee-tsoo-mohn)* based on the **e,** *(eh)* by filling in the blanks with the correct questions

prepositions. Choose the prepositions from those you have just learned.

Hon wa doko desu ka? *(hohn) (doh-koh)*
book where

Basu wa doko desu ka? *(bah-soo)*

Hon wa tēburu no _____ **desu.** *(tēh-boo-doo)*
table (P)

Basu wa hoteru no _____ **desu.** *(hoh-teh-doo)*
hotel (P)

☐ **hanmā** *(hahn-māh)*	hammer	_____
☐ **herikoputā** *(heh-dee-koh-poo-tāh)*	helicopter	_____
☐ **hiitā** *(hēē-tāh)*	heater	_____
☐ **hitto** *(heet-toh)*	hit	_____
☐ **hokkē** *(hohk-kēh)*	hockey	_____

(hi-doh) *(den-wah)* *(doh-koh)*
Haiiro no denwa wa doko desu ka?   **Aoi kāpetto wa doko desu ka?**
gray   (P) telephone (P) where   *(ah-oy)(kāh-pet-toh)*
                                        blue   carpet

E wa doko desu ka?
picture

(hi-doh) *(den-wah)* *(shee-doy)* *(kah-beh)* *(kah-kah-dee-mahss)*
Haiiro no denwa wa shiroi kabe _____ kakarimasu.
gray   (P) telephone white wall   hangs

(hi-doh) *(eh)*
Haiiro no denwa wa e no ___*tonari*___ desu.
gray   (P)   picture (P)

(koo-doy) *(tēh-boo-doo)*
Haiiro no denwa wa kuroi tēburu no _____ desu.
                         black   table   (P)

(ah-oy) *(kāh-pet-toh)* *(koo-doy)*
Aoi kāpetto wa kuroi tēburu no _____ desu.
blue   carpet   black   (P)

(eh) *(shee-doy)* *(kah-beh)*
E wa shiroi kabe _____ kakarimasu.
picture white wall

(shtah)
Ima, fill in each blank on the teahouse **shita** with the best possible preposition. The
                                            below

(koh-tah-eh)
correct **kotae** are at the bottom of the **pēji**. Have fun!
   answers

1. _____

2. *ni* _____

3. _____

4. _____

5. _____

6. _____

7. _____

8. _____

9. _____

KOTAE

	8. **shita**	6. **tonari**	
9. **kara**	7. **mae**	5. **aida**	3. **ushiro**	2. **ni**	1. **ue**
		4. **ni**	

27

Step 9

(shee-gah-tsoo) *(doh-koo-gah-tsoo)* *(koo-gah-tsoo)* *(jōō-ee-chee-gah-tsoo)* *(wah)* *(sahn-jōō-nee-chee)*
Shigatsu, Rokugatsu, Kugatsu to Jūichigatsu wa sanjūnichi desu . . .
April   June   September   and   November   (P)   30 days   have

Sound familiar? You have learned the **hi** *(hee)* of the **shūkan** *(shōō-kahn)*, so now it is time to learn the
        days   week

tsuki *(tsoo-kee)* of the **toshi** *(toh-shee)* and all the different kinds of **tenki** *(ten-kee)*. **Tatoeba** *(tah-toh-eh-bah)*, you ask about the **tenki** *(ten-kee)* in
months   year   weather   for example   weather

Nihongo just as you would in **Eigo** *(ay-goh)*: **"Kyō** *(kyōh)* **no tenki** *(ten-kee)* **wa dō** *(dōh)* **desu ka?"** Practice all the
                    English   today   (P)   weather   (P)   how is

possible answers to this **shitsumon** *(shee-tsoo-mohn)* and then write the following answers in the blanks below.
                   question

(kyōh)   *(ten-kee)*   *(dōh)*
Kyō no tenki wa dō desu ka?

(ah-tsee) *(dess)*
Kyō wa atsui desu. _____
    hot   is

(sah-moo-ee)
Kyō wa samui desu. _____
    cold

(ēē) *(ten-kee)*
Kyō wa ii tenki desu. *Kyō wa ii tenki desu.*
    good weather

(wah-doo-ee)(ten-kee)
Kyō wa warui tenki desu. _____
    bad   weather

(kyōh) *(ah-meh)* *(foo-dee-mahss)*
Kyō wa ame ga furimasu. _____
today   (P)   rain   (P)   falls

(yoo-kee)
Kyō wa yuki ga furimasu. _____
    snow

(kee-dee) (gah)(kah-kah-dee-mahss)
Kyō wa kiri ga kakarimasu. _____
    fog   (P)   hangs

(kah-zeh) *(foo-kee-mahss)*
Kyō wa kaze ga fukimasu. _____
    wind   (P)   blows

(tahn-goh)   *(soh-deh)(kah-dah)*   *(tsoo-kee)*
Ima, practice the **tango** on the next **pēji** aloud **sore kara** fill in the blanks with the **tsuki**
                                                and   then   month

(noh) (nah-mah-eh)   *(ten-kee)*
no namae and the appropriate **tenki** report. Notice that, in **Nihongo,** a number precedes
(P)   name   weather

           (gah-tsoo)   *(tah-toh-eh-bah)* *(sahn-gah-tsoo)*
the word for month, **gatsu.** **Tatoeba, Sangatsu** means third month or March.
               for example

☐ **hosuteru** *(hoh-soo-teh-doo)* . . . . hostel
☐ **hoteru** *(hoh-teh-doo)* . . . . hotel
☐ **hotto doggu** *(hoht-toh) (dohg-goo)* . . . . hot dog
☐ **hotto kēki** *(hoht-toh) (kēh-kee)* . . . . hot cake (pancake)
☐ **howaito sōsu** *(hoh-why-toh) (sōh-soo)* . . . white sauce

(ee-chee-gah-tsoo)
Ichigatsu _____
January

(yoo-kee) *(foo-dee-mahss)*
Ichigatsu ni wa yuki ga furimasu. _____
in (P) snow (P) falls

(nee-gah-tsoo)
Nigatsu _____
February

(moh)(yoo-kee) *(foo-dee-mahss)*
Nigatsu ni mo yuki ga furimasu. _____
in also snow (P) falls

(sahn-gah-tsoo)
Sangatsu _____
March

(ah-meh)
Sangatsu ni wa ame ga furimasu. _____
rain falls

(shee-gah-tsoo)
Shigatsu *Shigatsu*
April

(ah-meh)
Shigatsu ni mo ame ga furimasu. _____
also rain falls

(goh-gah-tsoo)
Gogatsu _____
May

(kah-zeh) *(foo-kee-mahss)*
Gogatsu ni wa kaze ga fukimasu. _____
wind blows

(doh-koo-gah-tsoo)
Rokugatsu _____
June

(moh)(kah-zeh) *(foo-kee-mahss)*
Rokugatsu ni mo kaze ga fukimasu. _____
also wind

(shee-chee-gah-tsoo)
Shichigatsu _____
July

(ah-tsee) (dess)
Shichigatsu ni wa atsui desu. _____
hot is

(hah-chee-gah-tsoo)
Hachigatsu _____
August

(ah-tsee)
Hachigatsu ni mo atsui desu. _____
also hot

(koo-gah-tsoo)
Kugatsu _____
September

(ten-kee) *(ee)*
Kugatsu ni wa tenki ga ii desu. _____
weather (P) good is

(jōō-gah-tsoo)
Jūgatsu _____
October

(kee-dee) *(kah-kah-dee-mahss)*
Jūgatsu ni wa kiri ga kakarimasu. _____
fog (P) hangs

(jōō-ee-chee-gah-tsoo)
Jūichigatsu _____
November

(sah-moo-ee)
Jūichigatsu ni wa samui desu. _____
cold

(jōō-nee-gah-tsoo)
Jūnigatsu _____
December

(ten-kee) *(wah-doo-ee)*
Jūnigatsu ni wa tenki ga warui desu. _____
weather bad

Ima, answer the following *(shee-tsoo-mohn)* **shitsumon** based on the *(eh)* **e** to the right.
questions   picture

(nee-gah-tsoo) *(ten-kee)* *(dōh)*
Nigatsu no tenki wa dō desu ka? _____
February (P) weather (P) how is

(shee-gah-tsoo)
Shigatsu no tenki wa dō desu ka? _____
April (P) weather how

(goh-gah-tsoo)
Gogatsu no tenki wa dō desu ka? _____
May (P)

(hah-chee-gah-tsoo)
Hachigatsu no tenki wa dō desu ka? _____
August (P)

(kyōh) *(ēē) (ten-kee)* *(wah-doo-ee)*
Kyō wa ii tenki desu ka? **Warui tenki desu ka?** _____
today (P) good weather is it   bad

☐ **imēji** *(ee-mēh-jee)* . . . . image _____
☐ **imitēshon** *(ee-mee-tēh-shohn)* . . . . imitation _____
☐ **inchi** *(een-chee)* . . . . inch _____
☐ **inku** *(een-koo)* . . . . ink _____
☐ **intabyū** *(een-tah-byōo)* . . . . interview _____

29

Now for the seasons of the **toshi** . . .
(toh-shee)
year

(foo-yoo)
fuyu
winter

(nah-tsoo)
natsu
summer

(ah-kee)
aki
autumn

(hah-doo)
haru
spring

fuyu

Fuyu wa

(sah-moo-ee)
samui desu.
cold   is

Natsu wa

(ah-tsee)
atsui desu.
hot

Aki wa

(ee)
ii tenki desu.
good

Haru wa

(ah-meh) *(foo-dee-mahss)*
ame ga furimasu.
rain   falls

At this point, it is a good time to familiarize yourself with **Nihon no kion.** Carefully read
                                                                   Japan (P) temperatures *(kee-ohn)*

the typical **tenki** forecasts **shita** and study the thermometer because temperatures in
            (ten-kee)   *(shtah)*
            weather   below

Nihon are calculated on the basis of Centigrade (not Fahrenheit).

(kah-shee) **kashi** Fahrenheit	*(sehs-shee)* **sesshi** Centigrade

212° F —— 100° C

(mee-zoo) *(foo-tōh)* *(soo-doo)*
mizu ga futtō suru
water (P) boils

98.6° F —— 37° C

(hay-neh-tsoo)
heinetsu
normal (body) temperature

(sahn-gah-tsoo)   *(foot-tsoo-kah)* *(geh-tsoo-yōh-bee)*   *(kee-ohn)*
Sangatsu no futsuka, Getsuyōbi no kion:
March   (P) second   Monday   (P) temperature

68° F —— 20° C

(sah-moo-ee)
samui
cold

(kōh-doo)
mizu ga kōru
freezes

32° F —— 0° C

(shee-oh) *(mee-zoo)*   *(kōh-doo)*
shio mizu ga kōru
salt water   freezes

(shee-chee-gah-tsoo)   *(ee-tsoo-kah)*(kah-yōh-bee)   *(kee-ohn)*
Shichigatsu no itsuka, Kayōbi no kion:
July   (P) fifth   Tuesday   (P) temperature

(ah-tsee)
atsui
hot

0° F —— -17.8° C

-10° F —— -23.3° C

☐ **jaketsu** *(jah-keh-tsoo)*	jacket	_____
☐ **jamu** *(jah-moo)*	jam	_____
☐ **jānarisuto** *(jāh-nah-dee-soo-toh)*	journalist	_____
☐ **janguru** *(jahn-goo-doo)*	jungle	_____
☐ **jazu** *(jah-zoo)*	jazz (music)	_____

(wah-gah-yah)
Wagaya
our home

In **Nihon,** not just the parents, but also the grandparents, aunts, uncles **to** cousins are
and
all considered as close family, so let's take a look at the **tango** for them. Study the family

(ah-tah-dah-shēē)
tree below and then write out the **atarashii tango** in the blanks on the next **pēji.** Notice
new

(nah-mah-eh)   (nah-nee)
that, in **Nihongo,** the family **namae** comes first, and the given **namae** (or **nani** we, in
name   what

(sahn)
Amerika, think of as the first **namae**) follows. Notice, on the following **pēji,** that **san**

is often used with the **namae** of relatives. It is simply a term of respect, meaning

"honorable."

(kah-zoh-koo) (say-doh)
Kazoku seido
family   system

Tanaka Hiroshi
Tanakasan (Mr. Tanaka)

Tanaka Kazuko
Tanaka Fujin (Mrs. Tanaka)

Tanaka Kazuo

Tanaka Michiko

Yamamoto Akira
Yamamotosan

Yamamoto Keiko
Yamamoto Fujin

(kah-zoh-koo)
kazoku
family

Tanaka Yoko

Tanaka Takashi

☐ **jerii** *(jeh-dēē)*........................	jelly	_____
☐ **jettoki** *(jet-toh-kee)*....................	jet airplane	_____
☐ **jinjāēru** *(jeen-jāh-ēh-doo)*.............	ginger ale	_____
☐ **jiipu** *(jēē-poo)*........................	jeep	_____
☐ **jirafu** *(jee-dah-foo)*....................	giraffe	_____

(soh-foo-boh) **sofubo** grandparents

(dyōh-sheen) **ryōshin** parents

(oh-jee-sahn) **ojiisan** _____
grandfather

(oh-tōh-sahn) (chee-chee) **otōsan / chichi** _____
father

(oh-bāh-sahn) **obāsan** _obāsan_
grandmother

(oh-kāh-sahn) (hah-hah) **okāsan / haha** _____
mother

(koh-doh-moh) **kodomo** children

(sheen-seh-kee) **shinseki** relatives

(moose-koh) **musuko** _____
son

(oh-jee-sahn) (oh-jee) **ojisan / oji** _____
uncle

(moo-soo-meh) **musume** _____
daughter

(oh-bah-sahn) (oh-bah) **obasan / oba** _____
aunt

(moose-koh)   (moo-soo-meh)   (oh-toh-koh) (kyōh-die)   (ohn-nah)   (kyōh-die)
Musuko to musume wa otoko no kyōdai to onna no kyōdai desu.
son   and   daughter   (P)   brother   (P)   and   sister   (P)   are

(nah-mah-eh)
Let's learn how to identify family members by **namae.** Study the following examples.
name

(oh-tōh-sahn)   (nah-mah-eh)   (nahn)
Otōsan no namae wa nan desu ka?
father   (P)   name   (P)   what is

Otōsan no namae wa _Kazuo_ **desu.**
(P)

(oh-kāh-sahn)   (nah-mah-eh)   (nahn)
Okāsan no namae wa nan desu ka?
mother   (P)   name   (P)   what is

Okāsan no namae wa _michiko_ **desu.**
(P)

(ee-mah)   *(eh)*
Ima you fill in the following blanks, based on the **e,** in the same manner.
now

(nah-mah-eh)
musuko **no namae wa nan desu ka?**
(P)   name   (P)   what is

_____ **no namae wa** _____ **desu.**
(P)

(nah-mah-eh)
Musume **no namae wa nan desu ka?**
(P)   name   (P)   what is

_____ **no namae wa** _____ **desu.**
(P)

☐ **kābu** *(kāh-boo)* .... curve _____
☐ **kādigan** *(kāh-dee-gahn)* .... cardigan _____
☐ **kādo** *(kāh-doh)* .... card _____
☐ **kafē** *(kah-fēh)* .... café, coffeehouse _____
32 ☐ **kafeteria** *(kah-feh-teh-dee-ah)* .... cafeteria

Daidokoro
kitchen

Study all the **e** *(eh)*
pictures on this **pēji** *(pēh-jee)* and then

practice saying and writing out the **tango.**

(koh-deh) *(die-doh-koh-doh)* *(dess)*
Kore wa daidokoro desu.
this (P) kitchen is

(day-zōh-koh)
reizōko
refrigerator

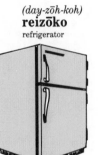

(gah-soo) *(dēn-jee)*
gasu **rēnji**
gas range

(boo-dōh-shoo)
budōshu
wine

(bēē-doo)
biiru
beer

(mee-doo-koo)
miruku
milk

(bah-tah)
bata
butter

miruku

(shee-tsoo-mohn)
Answer these **shitsumon** aloud.
questions

(bēē-doo) *(doh-koh)*
Biiru wa doko desu ka? .... **Biiru wa reizōko no naka desu.**
beer (P) where   refrigerator (P) inside
                                                 (day-zōh-koh) *(nah-kah)*

(mee-doo-koo)   *(boo-dōh-shoo)*
Miruku wa doko desu ka?   **Budōshu wa doko desu ka?**
milk   wine
(bah-tah)   *(oh-den-jee)* *(jōō-soo)*
Bata wa doko desu ka?   **Orenji jūsu wa doko desu ka?**
butter   orange juice

☐ **kāki** *(kāh-kee)* .... khaki
☐ **kamera** *(kah-meh-dah)* .... camera
☐ **kanbasu** *(kahn-bah-soo)* .... canvas
☐ **kānēshon** *(kāh-nēh-shohn)* .... carnation
☐ **kangarū** *(kahn-gah-dōo)* .... kangaroo

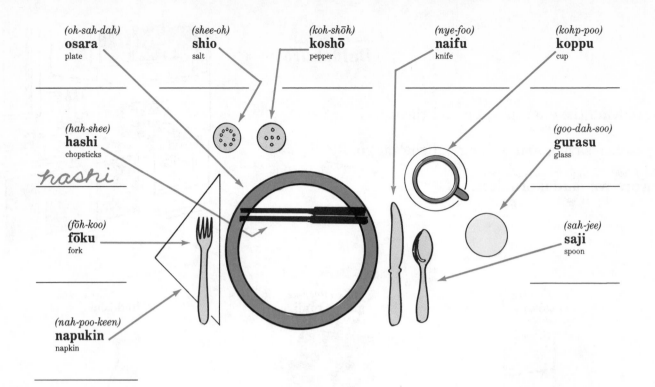

(oh-sah-dah)
osara
plate

_____

(shee-oh)
shio
salt

_____

(koh-shōh)
koshō
pepper

(nye-foo)
naifu
knife

_____

(kohp-poo)
koppu
cup

_____

(hah-shee)
hashi
chopsticks

hashi

(goo-dah-soo)
gurasu
glass

_____

(fōh-koo)
fōku
fork

_____

(sah-jee)
saji
spoon

_____

(nah-poo-keen)
napukin
napkin

_____

(shohk-kee-dah-nah)
shokkidana
cupboard

(pahn)
pan
bread

(oh-chah)
ocha
tea

(kōh-hēē)
kōhii
coffee

_____ _____ *pan* _____ _____

(pahn) *(doh-koh)*
Pan wa doko desu ka?
bread (P) where

(shohk-kee-dah-nah) *(nah-kah)*
Pan wa shokkidana no naka desu.
cupboard (P) inside

(oh-chah)
Ocha wa doko desu ka?
tea

(kōh-hēē)
Kōhii wa doko desu ka?
coffee
Now open your **hon** to the **pēji** with the labels and remove the
(hohn)
book

next **jūkyū mai** labels and proceed to label all these **mono** in your **daidokoro.** Do not
(jōō-kyōō)(my) nineteen (M)
(moh-noh) things
(die-doh-koh-doh) kitchen

forget to use every opportunity to say these **tango** out loud. **Kore wa hijō ni taisetsu desu.**
(koh-deh) this *(hee-jōh)* very (P) *(tie-seh-tsoo)* important

☐ **kanibaru** *(kah-nee-bah-doo)* . . . . carnival
☐ **kanū** *(kah-nōo)* . . . . canoe
☐ **kāpetto** *(kāh-pet-toh)* . . . . carpet
☐ **karā** *(kah-dāh)* . . . . collar
34 ☐ **karatto** *(kah-daht-toh)* . . . . carat

_____
_____
_____
_____
_____

In **Nihon,** there is not the wide variety of **shūkyō** that we find here in **Amerika.**
(shoo-kyōh)
religions

A person's **shūkyō** is usually one of the following.
(shoo-kyōh)
religion

1. **Shinkyō** *Shinkyō*
(sheen-kyōh)
Protestantism

2. **Katorikku** _____
(kah-toh-deek-koo)
Catholicism

3. **Bukkyō** _____
(book-kyōh)
Buddhism

4. **Shintō** _____
(sheen-tōh)
Shintoism

This is one of many **otera** in **Nihon.** You
(oh-teh-dah) *(nee-hohn)*
temples

will see several **otera** like this, as well as

jinja on your visit. You will notice that
(jeen-jah)
shrines

those who observe the **Shintō no shūkyō**
(sheen-tōh) *(shoo-kyōh)*
Shinto   (P)   religion

go to the **jinja** and those who observe the

Bukkyō no shūkyō go to the **otera.**
(book-kyōh)
Buddhist   (P)

Now let's learn how to say "I" in **Nihongo,** so you will be able to tell people

about yourself: I = **watashi** _____
(wah-tah-shee)

(wah-tah-shee) *(kah-toh-deek-koo)* *(dess)*
Watashi wa Katorikku desu. _____
I   (P)   Catholic   am

(wah-tah-shee) *(sheen-kyōh)* *(dess)*
Watashi wa Shinkyō desu. _____
I   Protestant   am

(ah-meh-dee-kah-jeen)
Watashi wa Amerikajin desu. _____
American

(nee-hohn-jeen)
Watashi wa Nihonjin desu. _____
Japanese

(nee)(ee-mahss)
Watashi wa Amerika ni imasu. _____
in   am

(nee)(ee-mahss)
Watashi wa Nihon ni imasu. _____
in   am

☐ **karē** *(kah-dēh)* .... curry _____
☐ **karendā** *(kah-den-dāh)* .... calendar _____
☐ **karifurawā** *(kah-dee-foo-dah-wāh)* .... cauliflower _____
☐ **karorii** *(kah-doh-dēē)* .... calorie _____
☐ **kashimia** *(kah-shee-mee-ah)* .... cashmere _____

35

(wah-tah-shee) *(kyōh-kai)* *(nee)* *(ee-mahss)*
Watashi wa kyōkai ni imasu. _____
I   church   in   am

(die-doh-koh-doh)
Watashi wa daidokoro ni imasu. _____
I   kitchen   in   am

(hah-hah)
Watashi wa haha desu. _____
I   mother   am

(chee-chee)
Watashi wa chichi desu. _____
I   father   am

(hoh-teh-doo) *(nee)* *(ee-mahss)*
Watashi wa hoteru ni imasu. _____
I   hotel   in   am

(dess-toh-dahn)
Watashi wa resutoran ni imasu. _____
              restaurant

(oh-bah)
Watashi wa oba desu. _____
              aunt

(oh-jee)
Watashi wa oji desu. _____
              uncle

(ee-mah)   *(hee-toh-bee-toh)*   *(eh)*   *(tah-dah-shēē)*
Ima identify all the **hitobito** in the **e** below by writing the **tadashii** **Nihongo no tango** for
now   people   picture   correct   Japanese   (P)   word

(hee-toh)
each **hito** on the line with the corresponding **bangō** under the **e.**
      person   *(bahn-gōh)*   *(eh)*
                                                                       number   picture

1. _____   2. _____

3. _____   4. _____

5. _ojisan_____   6. _____

7. _____

☐ **katarogu** *(kah-tah-doh-goo)* . . . . catalogue
☐ **Katorikku** *(kah-toh-deek-koo)* . . . . Catholic
☐ **kategorii** *(kah-teh-goh-dēē)* . . . . category
☐ **kāten** *(kāh-ten)* . . . . curtain
☐ **katto** *(kaht-toh)* . . . . cut

36

(nah-die-mahss)
Naraimasu
learn

(moht-teh) (ee-mahss) *(koo-dah-sigh) (dess)* *(ah-dee-mahss)* *(ee-mahss)*
You have already used the verbs **motte imasu, kudasai, desu, arimasu** and **imasu.**
have   please (give me) is   is   is

Although you might be able to "get by" with these verbs, let's assume you want to do

better than that. First, a quick review.

In **Nihongo,** how do you say "I" ? _____

Compare these two charts

(hee-jōh)
hijō ni carefully and learn these
very   (P)

six **tango** on the right.
(P)

	(wah-tah-shee)		*(wah-tah-shee-tah-chee)*
I =	**watashi**	we =	**watashitachi**
he =	*(kah-deh)* **kare**	you =	*(ah-nah-tah)* **anata**
she =	*(kah-noh-joh)* **kanojo**	they =	*(kah-deh-dah)* **karera**

(ay-goh) (toh) *(ah-nah-tah)*
Ima draw lines between the matching **Eigo to Nihongo no tango** below to see if **anata**
English   and   (P)   you

can keep these **tango** straight in your mind.

watashitachi	I
kare	you
karera	we
watashi	they
anata	she
kanojo	he

(ee-mah) (koh-noh) (hohn) *(den-shōō)* *(kah-mee)*
Ima close **kono hon** and write out both columns of the above **renshū** on a piece of **kami.**
now   this   book   practice   paper
(dōh) *(ēē) (wah-doo-ee)*
Dō did **anata** do? **Ii** or **warui?** **Ima** that **anata** know these **tango, anata** can say
how   good bad

almost anything in **Nihongo** with one basic formula: the "plug-in" formula. With this

formula, **anata wa** can correctly use any **tango** you wish.
          (P)

At the back of **kono hon, anata wa** will find **nana pēji** of flash cards to help **anata** learn

these **atarashii no tango.** Cut them out, carry them in your briefcase, purse, pocket or
              (P)

knapsack, and review them whenever **anata wa** have a free moment.

☐ **kēburu** *(keh-boo-doo)* .... cable   _____
— **kēburukā** *(kēh-boo-doo-kāh)* .... cable car   _____
☐ **kechappu** *(keh-chahp-poo)* .... ketchup   _____
☐ **kii** *(kēē)* .... key   _____
☐ **kinema** *(kee-nee-mah)* .... cinema   _____

37

To demonstrate, let's take six basic and practical verbs and see how the "plug-in" formula works. Write the verbs in the blanks **shita** after **anata** have practiced them out loud many times.

(hah-nah-shee-mahss)
hanashimasu = speak

(kye-mahss)
kaimasu = buy

(tie-zye) (shee-mahss)
taizai shimasu = stay

_____   *kaimasu*   _____

(chōō-mohn) (shee-mahss)
chūmon shimasu = order

(soon-deh) (ee-mahss)
sunde imasu = live

(yoh-bah-deh-teh) (ee-mahss)
yobarete imasu = be called

_____   _____   _____

Study the following patterns carefully — **anata wa** will see how easy **Nihongo** can be!

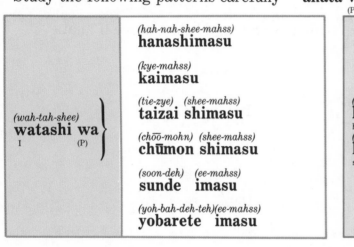

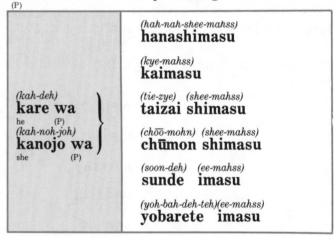

Note:
• Whether you are speaking about "I," "he," "she," "we" or "they," the same verb form is used in **Nihongo**. It's that easy!

• In **Nihongo**, "**tachi**" *(tah-chee)* is sometimes added to a word to indicate more than one person. **Tatoeba, watashi + tachi = watashitachi.**
(tah-toh-eh-bah)(wah-tah-shee) for example I   *(wah-tah-shee-tah-chee)* we

• Unlike **Eigo**, verbs are placed at the end of sentences in **Nihongo.**

• In **Nihongo**, "particle words," such as **wa**, are often placed after the subject.

□ **kiro** *(kee-doh)* .... kilo, kilometer   _____
□ **kōhii** *(kōh-hēē)* .... coffee   _____
□ **Koka Kōra** *(koh-kah) (kōh-dah)* .... Coca-Cola   _____
□ **kokku** *(kohk-koo)* .... cook   _____
38 □ **kokoa** *(koh-koh-ah)* .... cocoa   _____

Again, notice that **anata,** *(ah-nah-tah)* **watashitachi** *(wah-tah-shee-tah-chee)* and **karera** *(kah-deh-dah)* use the same verb form as **watashi,** *(wah-tah-shee)*
you   we   they   I

kare *(kah-deh)* and **kanojo.** *(kah-noh-joh)*
he   she

anata wa *(ah-nah-tah)* you (P) **watashitachi wa** *(wah-tah-shee-tah-chee)* we (P) **karera wa** *(kah-deh-dah)* they	} **hanashimasu** *(hah-nah-shee-mahss)* speak **kaimasu** *(kye-mahss)* buy **taizai shimasu** *(tie-zye) (shee-mahss)* stay

anata wa *(ah-nah-tah)* (P) **watashitachi wa** *(wah-tah-shee-tah-chee)* (P) **karera wa** *(kah-deh-dah)*	} **chūmon shimasu** *(chōo-mohn) (shee-mahss)* order **sunde imasu** *(soon-deh) (ee-mahss)* live **yobarete imasu** *(yoh-bah-deh-teh)(ee-mahss)* be called

Remember that verbs remain the same in **Nihongo.**

ex. **watashi wa kaimasu** *(kye-mahss)* (P) buy	**anata wa kaimasu** (P)
kare wa kaimasu	**watashitachi wa kaimasu**
kanojo wa kaimasu	**karera wa kaimasu**

In **Nihongo,** verbs are easy to learn. Fill in the following blanks with the verb shown.

Each time you write out the verb, be sure to say it aloud several times. **Kono renshū** *(den-shōo)* is
practice

hijō ni taisetsu. *(tie-seh-tsoo)* All the examples are practical to help **anata** as much as possible on your
(P) important

trip.

hanashimasu *(hah-nah-shee-mahss)*
speak

Watashi wa Nihongo o _____ .
(P)   (P)

Kare   **wa Eigo o** *hanashimasu* *(ay-goh)*
Kanojo (P)   English (P)

Anata wa Furansugo o _____ . *(foo-dahn-soo-goh)*
French

Watashitachi wa Chūgokugo o _____ . *(chōo-goh-koo-goh)*
Chinese

Karera wa Itariago o _____ . *(ee-tah-dee-ah-goh)*
Italian

kaimasu *(kye-mahss)*
buy

Watashi wa hon o *kaimasu* *(hohn)*
book

Kare   **wa sarada o** _____ . *(sah-dah-dah)*
Kanojo   salad

Anata wa jidōsha o _____ . *(jee-dōh-shah)*
car

Watashitachi wa tokei o _____ . *(toh-kay)*
clock

Karera wa ranpu o _____ . *(dahn-poo)*
lamp

(tie-zye) *(shee-mahss)*
taizai shimasu
stay

Watashi wa Nihon ni _____ .
(P) *(nee)* in

Kare wa Amerika ni _____ .
Kanojo (P) *(ah-meh-dee-kah)(nee)* in

Anata wa hoteru ni _____ .
(hoh-teh-doo) hotel

Watashitachi wa Ajia ni_____ .
(ah-jee-ah) Asia

Karera wa ie ni *taizai shimasu* .
(ee-eh) house

(soon-deh) *(ee-mahss)*
sunde imasu
live

Watashi wa Nihon ni _____ .
(P) *(nee)* in

Kare wa Amerika ni _____ .
Kanojo

Anata wa Furansu ni _____ .
(foo-dahn-soo) France

Watashitachi wa Supein ni _____ .
(soo-payn) Spain

Karera wa Doitsu ni _____ .
(doy-tsoo) Germany

Here are six more **dōshi**.
(dōh-shee) verbs

(chōō-mohn) *(shee-mahss)*
chūmon shimasu
order

Watashi wa ippai no mizu o _____ .
(P) *(eep-pie)* one glass (P) *(mee-zoo)* water (P)

Kare wa ippai no budōshu o _____ .
Kanojo *(eep-pie)* one glass (P) *(boo-dōh-shoo)* wine

Anata wa ippai no ocha o _____ .
(oh-chah) (P) tea

Watashitachi wa ippai no biiru o _____ .
(bēē-doo) (P) beer

Karera wa ippai no miruku o _____ .
(mee-doo-koo) (P) milk

(yoh-bah-deh-teh) *(ee-mahss)*
yobarete imasu
be called

Watashi wa Yoko to _____ .
(yoh-koh) *(toh)* (P)

Kare wa Suzukisan to _____ .
Kanojo *(soo-zoo-kee-sahn)* (P)

Anata wa Akira to _____ .
(ah-kee-dah)

Watashitachi wa Itosan to _____ .
(ee-toh-sahn)

Karera wa Yamamotosan to _____ .
(yah-mah-moh-toh -sahn)

*Notice how **san,** meaning "honorable," is combined with masculine and last names to show respect.

(kee-mahss)
kimasu = come

(ee-kee-mahss)
ikimasu = go

(nah-die-mahss)
naraimasu = learn

_____

_____

_____

(ee-dee-mahss)
irimasu = need

(hoh-shēē) (dess)
hoshii desu = would like

(moht-teh)(ee-mahss)
motte imasu = have

_____

hoshii desu

_____

Remember to say these **dōshi** out loud until **anata** have them down pat! Practice them,
(dōh-shee) verbs

write them out and use them in sentences of your own. The more **anata wa** practice **ima,**
(P)

the easier it will be later.

☐ **kone** *(koh-neh)* . . . . connection
☐ **konkuriito** *(kohn-koo-dēē-toh)* . . . . concrete
☐ **konpakuto kā** *(kohn-pah-koo-toh) (kāh)* . compact car
☐ **konpasu** *(kohn-pah-soo)* . . . . compass
☐ **konsāto** *(kohn-sāh-toh)* . . . . concert

_____
_____
_____
_____
_____

Think of how hard it would be to speak in **Eigo** *(ay-goh)* with no **dōshi** *(dōh-shee)* — it's the same in **Nihongo**.

(kee-mahss)
kimasu
come

Watashi wa Amerika kara _____ .
from *(kah-dah)*

Kare wa Nihon kara *kimasu* .
Kanojo   from *(kah-dah)*

Anata wa Doitsu kara _____ .
(doy-tsoo) Germany

Watashitachi wa Igirisu kara _____ .
(ee-gee-dee-soo) England

Karera wa Furansu kara _____ .
(foo-dahn-soo) France

(nah-die-mahss)
naraimasu
learn

Watashi wa Nihongo o _____ .
(P)

Kare wa Eigo o _____ .
Kanojo

Anata wa Itariago o _____ .
(ee-tah-dee-ah-goh) Italian

Watashitachi wa Furansugo o _____ .
(foo-dahn-soo-goh) French

Karera wa Chūgokugo o _____ .
(chōo-goh-koo-goh) Chinese

(moht-teh) (ee-mahss)
motte imasu
have

Watashi wa hyaku en o _____ .
(hyah-koo) (en)
100   yen (P)

Kare wa gohyaku en o _____ .
Kanojo *(goh-hyah-koo) (en)*
500   yen (P)

Anata wa sen en o _____ .
(sen)
1000

Watashitachi wa gosen en o _____ .
(goh-sen)
5000

Karera wa ichiman en o _____ .
(ee-chee-mahn)
10,000

(ee-kee-mahss)
ikimasu
go

Watashi wa Nihon e _____ .
(eh)
to

Kare wa Amerika e _____ .
Kanojo *(eh)*
to

Anata wa Supein e *ikimasu* .
(soo-payn) Spain

Watashitachi wa Yōroppa e _____ .
(yōh-dohp-pah) Europe

Karera wa Igirisu e _____ .
(ee-gee-dee-soo)

(ee-dee-mahss)
irimasu
need

Watashi wa ippai no budōshu ga ____ .
(eep-pie) *(boo-dōh-shoo)*
one glass (P)   (P)

Kare wa ippai no ocha ga _____ .
Kanojo *(eep-pie)* *(oh-chah)*
one glass (P) tea

Anata wa ippai no mizu ga _____ .
(mee-zoo)
(P)   water

Watashitachi wa ippai no kōhii ga ___ .
(kōh-hēē)

Karera wa ippai no miruku ga _____ .
(mee-doo-koo) milk

(hoh-shēē) (dess)
hoshii desu
would like

Watashi wa ippai no budōshu ga ____ .
(eep-pie) *(boo-dōh-shoo)* *(gah)*
one glass (P) wine   (P)

Kare wa ippai no mizu ga _____ .
Kanojo *(eep-pie)* *(mee-zoo)*
one glass (P) water (P)

Anata wa ippai no miruku ga _____ .
(mee-doo-koo)
(P)

Watashitachi wa ippai no kōhii ga ___ .
(kōh-hēē)
(P)   coffee

Karera wa ippai no ocha ga _____ .
(oh-chah)
(P)   tea

☐ **konsome** *(kohn-soh-meh)* . . . . consommé _____
☐ **konsutāche** *(kohn-soo-tāh-cheh)* . . . . cornstarch _____
☐ **kontakuto renzu** *(kohn-tah-koo-toh) (den-zoo)* . . . contact lens _____
☐ **kontena** *(kohn-teh-nah)* . . . . container _____
☐ **kontorasuto** *(kohn-toh-dah-soo-toh)* . . . . contrast _____

41

Ima take a deep breath. See if **anata wa** can fill in the blanks **shita**. The correct *(koh-tah-eh)* **kotae**
answers
are at the bottom of *(koh-noh)* **kono** *(pēh-jee)* **pēji.**
this   page

1. I speak Japanese. _____

2. He comes from America. *Kare wa Amerika kara kimasu.*

3. We learn Japanese. _____

4. You have 10 yen. _____

5. She needs a glass of water. _____

6. We would like a room. _____

7. I am called Yoko. _____

8. They live in America. _____

9. She buys a book. _____

10. He orders a beer. _____

(eh)
Ee, it is hard to get used to all those particle words. But don't give up. Just keep it up
yes
and before **anata wa** know it, you'll be using them naturally.

In the following Steps, **anata wa** will be introduced to more and more *(dōh-shee)* **dōshi** and **anata wa**
verbs
should drill them in exactly the same way as **anata** did in this section. Look up the
(ah-tah-dah-shēē)
atarashii tango in your *(jee-bee-kee)* **jibiki** and make up your own sentences using the same type of
new   dictionary
pattern. Always try out your *(ah-tah-dah-shēē)* **atarashii tango** for that's how you make them yours to use
new
on your holiday. Remember, the more **anata** practice, the more enjoyable your trip will be.

Good luck!

Be sure to check off your free **tango** in the box provided as you learn each one. ☑

KOTAE

10. **Kare wa biiru o chūmon shimasu.**	5. **Kanojo wa ippai no mizu ga irimasu.**
9. **Kanojo wa hon o kaimasu.**	4. **Anata wa jū en o motte imasu.**
8. **Karera wa Amerika ni sunde imasu.**	3. **Watashitachi wa Nihongo o naraimasu.**
7. **Watashi wa Yoko to yobarete imasu.**	2. **Kare wa Amerika kara kimasu.**
6. **Watashitachi wa heya ga hoshii desu.**	1. **Watashi wa Nihongo o hanashimasu.**

42

(jee-kahn)
Jikan
time

Anata wa know how to tell the *(hee)* **hi** of the *(shōō-kahn)* **shūkan** *(toh)* **to** the *(tsoo-kee)* **tsuki** of the *(toh-shee)* **toshi,** so now let's
days   week   and   months   year

learn to tell time. As a traveler in **Nihon, anata wa** need to be able to tell time in order to

make *(yoy-yah-koo)* **yoyaku** and to catch *(den-shah)* **densha.** Here are the "basics."
reservations   trains

What time is it? = *(nahn-jee)* **Nanji desu ka?**
what time is it

_____

before = *(my)* **mae** _mae_

after = *(soo-gee)* **sugi** _____

half = *(hahn)* **han** _____

(goh-jee) **Goji desu.**
five o'clock

(sahn-jee) **Sanji desu.**
three o'clock

(yoh-jee)(hahn) **Yoji han desu.**
four   (+) half

(nee-jee)(hahn) **Niji han desu.**
two   (+) half

(hah-chee-jee) (nee-jip-poon) **Hachiji nijippun desu.**   OR
eight o'clock 20 minutes

(nee-jip-poon) (soo-gee) **Hachiji nijippun sugi desu.**
eight o'clock 20 minutes after

(hah-chee-jee) (nee-jip-poon) (my) **Hachiji nijippun mae desu.**   OR
eight o'clock 20 minutes before

(shee-chee-jee) (yohn-jip-poon) (soo-gee) **Shichiji yonjippun (sugi) desu.**
seven o'clock 40 minutes after

Ima fill in the blanks according to the *(jee-kahn)* **jikan** indicated on the *(toh-kay)* **tokei.** *(koh-tah-eh)* **Kotae wa**
time   clocks   answers

shita ni arimasu.

_____ desu.   _Ichiji han_ desu.

_____ desu.   _____ desu.

_____ desu.   _____ desu.

_____ desu.   _____ desu.

KOTAE	
Rokuji jippun mae desu.	Rokuji jippun (sugi) desu.
Jūniji nijippun (sugi) desu.	Shichiji han desu.
Yoji desu.	Niji nijippun (sugi) desu.
Ichiji han desu.	Jūji jippun (sugi) desu.

Here are more time-telling **tango** to add to your **tango** power.

words   word

(jōō-goh-foon)
jūgofun = a quarter/15 minutes

(jōō-goh-foon)(my)
jūgofun mae = a quarter before

(jōō-goh-foon) (soo-gee)
jūgofun sugi = a quarter after

(nee-jee) (jōō-goh-foon)(soo-gee)
Niji jūgofun sugi desu.
two o'clock quarter   after

OR

(jōō-goh-foon)
Niji jūgofun desu.
15 minutes

(nee-jee)   *(my)*
Niji jūgofun mae desu.
two   before

OR

(ee-chee-jee)(yohn-jōō-goo-foon)
Ichiji   yonjūgofun desu.
one o'clock   45 minutes

Now it is your turn.

_____ desu.

_____ desu.

_____ desu.

_____ desu.

(tie-seh-tsoo)   *(bahn-gōh)*   *(shee-tsoo-mohn)*
See how **taisetsu** learning **bangō** is? **Ima** answer the following **shitsumon** based on the
          important   numbers   questions
(toh-kay)   *(koh-noh) (pēh-jee)*
tokei below. **Kotae** are at the bottom of **kono pēji.**

| **Nanji desu ka?** |

1

2

3

1. _____

2. _____

3. _____

4. *Ichiji han desu.*

5. _____

6. _____

7. _____

KOTAE

7. Niji jūgofun sugi desu.
6. Kuji nijippun sugi desu.
5. Jūniji jūgofun sugi desu.

4. Ichiji han desu.
3. Hachiji desu.
2. Shichiji han desu.
1. Rokuji desu.

When **anata wa** answer an "**itsu**" *(ee-tsoo)* question, say "**ni**" *(nee)* after you give the time.

When   when   at

(den-shah)   *(ee-tsoo)(kee-mahss)*
Densha wa itsu kimasu ka? <u>Rokuji ni kimasu.</u>
train   when   comes

電車 6:00

Ima answer the following **shitsumon** *(shee-tsoo-mohn)* based on the **tokei** *(toh-kay)* below. Be sure to practice saying
questions

each **shitsumon** *(shee-tsoo-mohn)* out loud several times.
question

(kohn-sāh-toh)   *(ee-tsoo)(hah-jee-mah-dee-mahss)*
Konsāto wa itsu hajimarimasu ka? _____
concert   when   begin

(ay-gah)   *(hah-jee-mah-dee-mahss)*
Eiga wa itsu hajimarimasu ka? _____
movie   begin

(kēē-doy) (bah-soo)   *(kee-mahss)*
Kiiroi basu wa itsu kimasu ka? _____
yellow   bus   come

(tah-koo-shēē)   *(kee-mahss)*
Takushii wa itsu kimasu ka? _____
taxi   come

(dess-toh-dahn)   *(ah-kee-mahss)*
Resutoran wa itsu akimasu ka? <u>Goji ni akimasu.</u>
restaurant   open

(shee-mah-dee-mahss)
Resutoran wa itsu shimarimasu ka? _____
closed

(ah-sah)   *(hah-chee-jee)*
Asa no hachiji ni wa,
morning (P)   eight o'clock
(oh-hi-yōh) (goh-zye-mahss)   *(toh) (ēē-mahss)*
"Ohayō gozaimasu" to iimasu.
good morning   (P)   one says

(bahn)   *(shee-chee-jee)*
Ban no shichiji ni wa,
evening (P)   seven o'clock
(kohn-bahn) (wah)   *(ēē-mahss)*
"Konban wa" to iimasu."
good evening   (P)

(goh-goh)   *(ee-chee-jee)*
Gogo no ichiji ni wa,
afternoon   one o'clock
(kohn-nee-chee)   *(ēē-mahss)*
"Konnichi wa" to iimasu.""
good afternoon   (P)   one says

(yoh-doo)   *(jōō-jee)*
Yoru no jūji ni wa,
night   (P)   10 o'clock
(oh-yah-soo-mee-nah-sigh)   *(ēē-mahss)*
"Oyasuminasai" to iimasu.""
good night   (P)

☐ **kontorōru** *(kohn-toh-dōh-doo)* .... control
☐ **kopii** *(koh-pēē)* .... copy
☐ **koppu** *(kohp-poo)* .... cup, glass
☐ **kōrasu** *(kōh-dah-soo)* .... chorus
☐ **korekushon** *(koh-deh-koo-shohn)* .... collection

45

Remember:

What time is it? =	*(nahn-jee)* **Nanji desu ka?**

When/at what time =	*(ee-tsoo)* **Itsu?** *(nahn-jee)(nee)* **Nanji ni?**

Can you pronounce and understand

the following paragraph?

(koh-noh) *(den-shah)*
Kono densha wa Tōkyō ni sanji

(tsoo-kee-mahss) *(ee-mah)*
jūgofun ni tsukimasu. Ima sanji
at   arrives   now

nijippun desu. Densha wa

(oh-koo-deh-teh) *(kyōh)*
okurete imasu. Kyō sono densha
late   today

(tsoo-kee-mahss)
wa goji jūgofun ni tsukimasu.
arrives

(ah-shtah)
Ashita densha wa sanji jūgofun
tomorrow

ni tsukimasu.

(koh-koh)   *(shee-tsoo-mohn)*
Koko ni some more practice exercises **ga arimasu.** Answer the **shitsumon** based on the
questions
(jee-kahn) (P)
jikan given below.
time

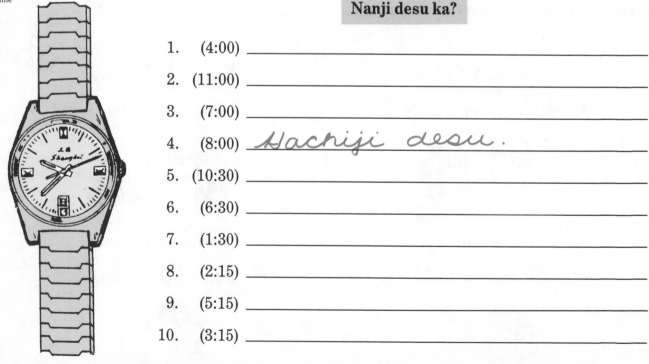

Nanji desu ka?

1. (4:00) _____

2. (11:00) _____

3. (7:00) _____

4. (8:00) *Hachiji desu.*

5. (10:30) _____

6. (6:30) _____

7. (1:30) _____

8. (2:15) _____

9. (5:15) _____

10. (3:15) _____

☐ **koruku** *(koh-doo-koo)*	cork	_____
☐ **kōsu** *(kōh-soo)*	course	_____
☐ **kosuto** *(koh-soo-toh)*	cost	_____
☐ **kōto** *(kōh-toh)*	coat	_____
☐ **kukkii** *(kook-kēē)*	cookie	_____

46

Here is a quick quiz. Fill in the blanks with the **tadashii tango**. *(tah-dah-shee)* **Kotae** *(koh-tah-eh)* are below.
correct *answers*

1. **Ippun wa** *(eep-poon) (wah)* _____ **byō desu.** *(byōh) (dess)*
   one minute (M) (?) seconds has

2. **Ichijikan wa** *(ee-chee-jee-kahn)* _____ **pun desu.** *(poon)*
   one hour (?) minutes

3. **Ichinichi wa** *(ee-chee-nee-chee)* _____ **jikan desu.** *(jee-kahn)*
   one day (?) hours

4. **Isshūkan wa** *(eesh-shōō-kahn)* *nana* _____ **nichi desu.** *(nee-chee)*
   one week (?) days

5. **Ikkagetsu wa** *(eek-kah-geh-tsoo)* _____ **nichi desu.** *(nee-chee)*
   one month (?) days

6. **Ichinen wa** *(ee-chee-nen)* _____ **kagetsu desu.** *(kah-geh-tsoo)*
   one year (?) months

7. **Ichinen wa** *(ee-chee-nen)* _____ **shūkan desu.** *(shōō-kahn)*
   one year (?) weeks

8. **Ichinen wa** _____ **nichi desu.** *(nee-chee)*
   (?) days

Here is a sample **pēji** from a **Nihon no densha no jikokuhyo.** *(jee-koh-koo-hyoh)* **Tokkyū ressha wa** *(tohk-kyōō) (desh-shah)*
(P) train (P) schedule special express train

hijō ni hayai desu. *(hee-jōh) (hi-yi)* **Kyūkō ressha wa hayai desu.** *(kyōō-kōh) (desh-shah) (hi-yi)* **Futsū ressha wa osoi desu.** *(foo-tsōō) (oh-soy)*
very fast express train fast local/ordinary slow

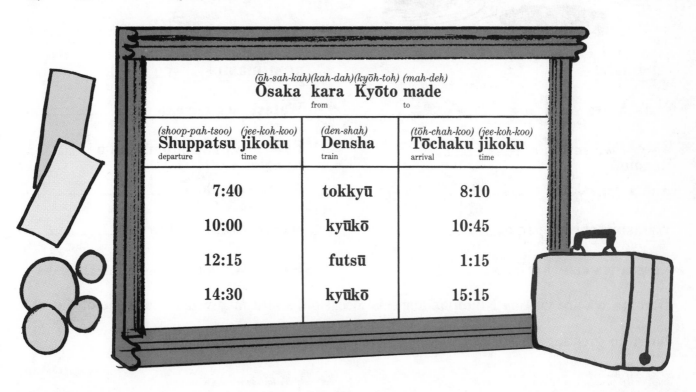

(ōh-sah-kah)(kah-dah)(kyōh-toh) (mah-deh) Ōsaka kara Kyōto made		
from	to	
Shuppatsu jikoku *(shoop-pah-tsoo) (jee-koh-koo)* departure time	**Densha** *(den-shah)* train	**Tōchaku jikoku** *(tōh-chah-koo) (jee-koh-koo)* arrival time
7:40	tokkyū	8:10
10:00	kyūkō	10:45
12:15	futsū	1:15
14:30	kyūkō	15:15

KOTAE

1. rokujū
2. rokujū
3. nijūyo
4. nana
5. sanjū
6. jūni
7. gojūni
8. sanbyaku rokujū go

47

Here are some **atarashii** *(ah-tah-dah-shēē)* **dōshi** *(dōh-shee)* for Step 12.
  new   verbs

iimasu *(ēē-mahss)* = say   **tabemasu** *(tah-beh-mahss)* = eat   **nomimasu** *(noh-mee-mahss)* = drink

_____   *tabemasu*   _____

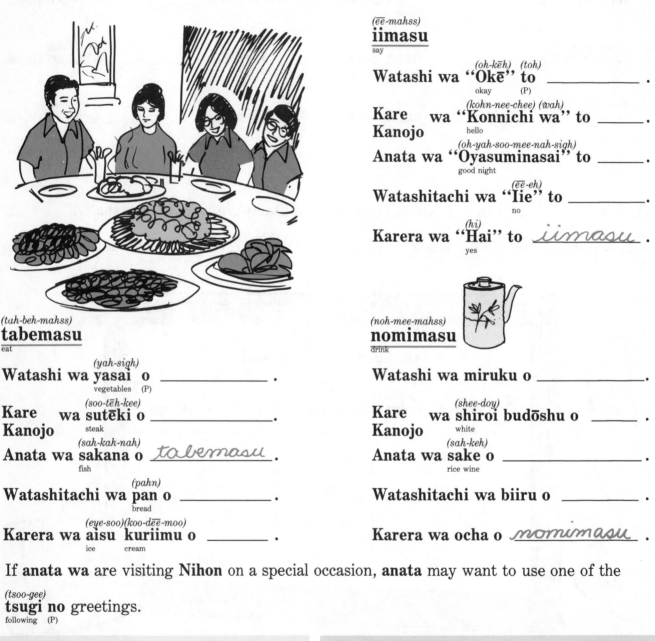

iimasu *(ēē-mahss)*
say

Watashi wa "Okē" to _____ .
       okay *(oh-kēh)* *(toh)* (P)

Kare
Kanojo wa "Konnichi wa" to _____ .
       (kohn-nee-chee) (vah) hello

Anata wa "Oyasuminasai" to _____ .
       (oh-yah-soo-mee-nah-sigh) good night

Watashitachi wa "Iie" to _____ .
                    (ēē-eh) no

Karera wa "Hai" to *iimasu* .
          (hi) yes

tabemasu *(tah-beh-mahss)*
eat

Watashi wa yasai o _____ .
        (yah-sigh) vegetables (P)

Kare
Kanojo wa sutēki o _____ .
       (soo-tēh-kee) steak

Anata wa sakana o *tabemasu* .
       (sah-kah-nah) fish

Watashitachi wa pan o _____ .
               (pahn) bread

Karera wa aisu kuriimu o _____ .
       (eye-soo)(koo-dēē-moo) ice   cream

nomimasu *(noh-mee-mahss)*
drink

Watashi wa miruku o _____ .

Kare
Kanojo wa shiroi budōshu o _____ .
       (shee-doy) white

Anata wa sake o _____ .
       (sah-keh) rice wine

Watashitachi wa biiru o _____ .

Karera wa ocha o *nomimasu* .

If **anata wa** are visiting **Nihon** on a special occasion, **anata** may want to use one of the

tsugi no greetings.
(tsoo-gee)
following (P)

Merii kurisumasu *(meh-dee)(koo-dee-soo-mahss)* = Merry Christmas	**Omedetō gozaimasu** *(oh-meh-deh-tōh)(goh-zye-mahss)* = Congratulations
Otanjōbi omedetō gozaimasu *(oh-tahn-jōh-bee)* = Happy Birthday	**Akemashite omedetō gozaimasu** *(ah-keh-mah-shtay)* = Happy New Year

☐ **māchi** *(māh-chee)* .... march   _____
☐ **machinē** *(mah-chee-nēh)* .... matinée   _____
☐ **madamu** *(mah-dah-moo)* .... madam   _____
☐ **magajin** *(mah-gah-jeen)* .... magazine   _____
☐ **māgarin** *(māh-gah-deen)* .... margarine   _____

48

(eh) **e**	*(ee-mah)* **ima**	*(koo)* **9 ku**	*(kohn-nee-chee)* *(wah)* **konnichi wa**
(ten-jōh) **tenjō**	*(shah-koh)* **shako**	*(jōō)* **10 jū**	*(kohn-bahn)* *(wah)* **konban wa**
(kah-doh) **kado**	*(chee-kah)* **chika**	*(shee-doy)* **shiroi**	*(oh-yah-soo-mee-nah-sigh)* **oyasuminasai**
(mah-doh) **mado**	*(jee-dōh-shah)* **jidōsha**	*(koo-doy)* **kuroi**	*(day-zōh-koh)* **reizōko**
(dahn-poo) **ranpu**	*(jee-ten-shah)* **jitensha**	*(kēē-doy)* **kiiroi**	*(gah-soo)* *(dēn-jee)* **gasu rēnji**
(den-tōh) **dentō**	*(ee-noo)* **inu**	*(ah-kye)* **akai**	*(boo-dōh-shoo)* **budōshu**
(soh-fāh) **sofā**	*(neh-koh)* **neko**	*(ah-oy)* **aoi**	*(bēē-doo)* **biiru**
(ee-soo) **isu**	*(nee-wah)* **niwa**	*(hi-doh)* **haiiro**	*(mee-doo-koo)* **miruku**
(kāh-pet-toh) **kāpetto**	*(yōō-bean)* **yūbin**	*(chi-doh)* **chairo**	*(bah-tah)* **bata**
(tēh-boo-doo) **tēburu**	*(yōō-bean-bah-koh)* **yūbinbako**	*(mee-doh-dee)* **midori**	*(oh-sah-dah)* **osara**
(doh-ah) **doa**	*(hah-nah)* **hana**	*(moh-moh-ee-doh)* **momoiro**	*(shee-oh)* **shio**
(toh-kay) **tokei**	*(yoh-bee-deen)* **yobirin**	*(oh-den-jee)* **orenji**	*(koh-shōh)* **koshō**
(kāh-ten) **kāten**	*(ee-chee)* **1 ichi**	*(nee-chee-yōh-bee)* **Nichiyōbi**	*(nye-foo)* **naifu**
(kah-beh) **kabe**	*(nee)* **2 ni**	*(geh-tsoo-yōh-bee)* **Getsuyōbi**	*(kohp-poo)* **koppu**
(ee-eh) **ie**	*(sahn)* **3 san**	*(kah-yōh-bee)* **Kayōbi**	*(oh-hah-shee)* **ohashi**
(shoh-sigh) **shosai**	*(shee)* **4 shi**	*(soo-ee-yōh-bee)* **Suiyōbi**	*(fōh-koo)* **fōku**
(foo-doh-bāh) **furobā**	*(goh)* **5 go**	*(moh-koo-yōh-bee)* **Mokuyōbi**	*(goo-dah-soo)* **gurasu**
(die-doh-koh-doh) **daidokoro**	*(doh-koo)* **6 roku**	*(keen-yōh-bee)* **Kinyōbi**	*(nah-poo-keen)* **napukin**
(sheen-shee-tsoo) **shinshitsu**	*(shee-chee)* **7 shichi**	*(doh-yōh-bee)* **Doyōbi**	*(sah-jee)* **saji**
(chah-noh-mah) **chanoma**	*(hah-chee)* **8 hachi**	*(oh-hi-yōh)* *(goh-zye-mahss)* **ohayō gozaimasu**	*(shohk-kee-dah-nah)* **shokkidana**

STICKY LABELS

This book has over 150 special sticky labels for you to use as you learn new words. When you are introduced to a word, remove the corresponding label from these pages. Be sure to use each of these unique labels by adhering them to a picture, window, lamp, or whatever object it refers to. The sticky labels make learning to speak Japanese much more fun and a lot easier than you ever expected.

For example, when you look in the mirror and see the label, say

(kah-gah-mee)
"kagami."

Don't just say it once, say it again and again.

And once you label the refrigerator, you should never again open that door without saying

(day-zōh-koh)
"reizōko."

By using the sticky labels, you not only learn new words but friends and family learn along with you!

(pahn) **pan**	*(hah-gah-kee)* **hagaki**	*(hah-mee-gah-kee)* **hamigaki**	*(sōō-tsoo)* **sūtsu**
(oh-chah) **ocha**	*(keet-teh)* **kitte**	*(kah-mee-soh-dee)* **kamisori**	*(neh-koo-tie)* **nekutai**
(kōh-chah) **kōcha**	*(hohn)* **hon**	*(deh-oh-doh-dahn-toh)* **deodoranto**	*(hahn-kah-chee)* **hankachi**
(kōh-hēē) **kōhii**	*(zahss-shee)* **zasshi**	*(koo-shee)* **kushi**	*(shah-tsoo)* **shatsu**
(bed-doh) **beddo**	*(sheen-boon)* **shinbun**	*(ōh-bāh)* **ōbā**	*(jah-keh-tsoo)* **jaketsu**
(kah-keh-boo-tohn) **kakebuton**	*(meh-gah-neh)* **megane**	*(dayn-kōh-toh)* **reinkōto**	*(zoo-bohn)* **zubon**
(mah-koo-dah) **makura**	*(teh-deh-bee)* **terebi**	*(kah-sah)* **kasa**	*(doh-deh-soo)* **doresu**
(meh-zah-mah-shee) *(doh-kay)* **mezamashi dokei**	*(goh-mee-bah-koh)* **gomibako**	*(teh-boo-koo-doh)* **tebukuro**	*(boo-dow-soo)* **burausu**
(yōh-foo-koo) *(dahn-soo)* **yōfuku dansu**	*(pah-soo-pōh-toh)* **pasupōto**	*(bōh-shee)* **bōshi**	*(soo-kāh-toh)* **sukāto**
(sen-men-die) **senmendai**	*(keep-poo)* **kippu**	*(nah-gah-goo-tsoo)* **nagagutsu**	*(sēh-tāh)* **sētā**
(shah-wāh) **shawā**	*(sōō-tsoo-kēh-soo)* **sūtsukēsu**	*(koo-tsoo)* **kutsu**	*(boo-dah-jāh)* **burajā**
(toy-deh) **toire**	*(hahn-doh-bahg-goo)* **handobaggu**	*(koo-tsoo-shtah)* **kutsushita**	*(soo-deep-poo)* **surippu**
(kah-gah-mee) **kagami**	*(sigh-foo)* **saifu**	*(pahn-tāy)* *(soo-tohk-keen-goo)* **panteii sutokkingu**	*(pahn-tāy)* **panteii**
(tah-oh-doo) **taoru**	*(oh-kah-neh)* **okane**	*(pah-jah-mah)* **pajama**	*(hah-dah-gee)* **hadagi**
(teh-noo-goo-ee) **tenugui**	*(kah-meh-dah)* **kamera**	*(nye-toh-gown)* **naitogaun**	*(oh-shoh-koo-jee) (oh) (dōh-zoh)* **Oshokuji o dōzo!**
(yoo-ah-gah-dee) *(tah-oh-doo)* **yuagari taoru**	*(fee-doo-moo)* **firumu**	*(bah-soo-dōh-boo)* **basurōbu**	*(koo-dah-sigh)* **kudasai**
(en-pee-tsoo) **enpitsu**	*(mee-zoo-gee)* **mizugi**	*(soo-deep-pah)* **surippa**	*(shee-tsoo-day)* **shitsurei**
(pen) **pen**	*(sahn-dah-doo)* **sandaru**	*(wah-tah-shee) (wah)* *(ah-meh-dee-kah-jeen)* *(dess)* **Watashi wa Amerikajin desu.**	
(kah-mee) **kami**	*(sek-ken)* **sekken**	*(nee-hohn-goh) (oh)* *(nah-die-mahss)* **Nihongo o naraimasu.**	
(teh-gah-mee) **tegami**	*(hah-boo-dah-shee)* **haburashi**	*(nah-mah-eh) (wah)* *(dess)* **Namae wa _____ desu.** *(last name)*	

PLUS . . .

Your book includes a number of other innovative features. At the back of the book, you'll find seven pages of flash cards. Cut them out and flip through them at least once a day.

On pages 112 and 113, you'll find a beverage guide and a menu guide. Don't wait until your trip to use them. Clip out the menu guide and use it tonight at the dinner table. And use the beverage guide to practice ordering your favorite drinks.

By using the special features in this book, you will be speaking Japanese before you know it.

(tah-noh-sheen-deh)
Tanoshinde kudasai.
have fun

(hee-gah-shee)	*(nee-shee)*	*(mee-nah-mee)*	*(kee-tah)*
Higashi -	**Nishi,**	**Minami** -	**Kita**
east	west	south	north

While in **Nihon, anata wa** will probably use a **chizu** *(chee-zoo)* to find your way around. Study the
(P) map

direction **tango** below until **anata** are familiar with them and can recognize them on your

(chee-zoo)
chizu of **Nihon.**
map

(hee-gah-shee)	*(nee-shee)*	*(mee-nah-mee)*	*(kee-tah)*
higashi	**nishi**	**minami**	**kita**
east	west	south	north

Anata wa will also see the following pictograms used to express **hōkō** *(hōh-kōh)* in **Nihon:**
directions

東 = east   西 = west   南 = south   北 = north.

Ima practice these new direction **tango!**

(hee-gah-shee)			
higashi	=	the east	_____
(nee-shee) **nishi**	=	the west	_____
(mee-nah-mee) **minami**	=	the south	_____
(kee-tah) **kita**	=	the north	*kita*

(hee-gah-shee) (noh)			
higashi no	=	eastern	_____
(P)			
(nee-shee) **nishi no**	=	western	_____
(P)			
(mee-nah-mee) **minami no**	=	southern	_____
(P)			
(kee-tah) **kita no**	=	northern	_____
(P)			

In **Nihon** these **tango wa hijō ni taisetsu desu.** Learn them **kyō**! But what about more
(hee-jōh) *(tie-seh-tsoo)* *(kyōh)*
very   important   today

basic **hōkō** *(hōh-kōh)* such as "left," "right," and "straight ahead"? Let's learn these **tango.**
directions

(hee-dah-dee)
hidari
left

(mee-gee)
migi
right

	(hee-dah-dee) (nee)
to the left =	**hidari ni**
	(mee-gee) (nee)
to the right =	**migi ni**
	(mahss-soo-goo)
straight ahead =	**massugu**

☐ **maikurohon** *(my-koo-doo-hohn)*	microphone	_____
☐ **mainasu** *(my-nah-soo)*	minus	_____
☐ **mairu** *(my-doo)*	mile	_____
☐ **majikku** *(mah-jeek-koo)*	magic	_____
☐ **makaroni** *(mah-kah-doh-nee)*	macaroni	_____

49

Just as in **Eigo,** the following **tango** go a long way. **Anata wa** can't practice them enough.

words

(koo-dah-sigh) **kudasai**	=	please _____
(ah-dee-gah-tōh)(goh-zye-mahss) **arigatō gozaimasu**	=	thank you _____
(shee-tsoo-day) **shitsurei**	=	excuse me *shitsurei* _____

(koh-koh)   *(kye-wah)*
Koko ni are two typical **kaiwa** for someone who is trying to find something.
here   (P)   conversations

Suzukisan: *(shee-tsoo-day)*   *(gah)(tay-koh-koo)*
Shitsurei desu ga Teikoku Hoteru wa doko desu ka?
excuse me   but imperial   where   is

Itosan: *(mōh)* *(choh)* *(eh)(ee-kee-mahss)* *(nee-bahn-meh)*   *(mee-chee)* *(hee-dah-dee)* *(mah-gah-dee-mahss)*
Mō ni cho e ikimasu. Nibanme no michi de hidari ni magarimasu.
more   blocks (P) go   second   (P) street   to the left   turn

Suzukisan: *(shee-tsoo-day)*   *(gah)(oo-eh-noh) (bee-joo-tsoo-kahn)*
Shitsurei desu ga Ueno Bijutsukan wa doko desu ka?
excuse me   but   museum

Itosan: *(koh-koh)*   *(mee-gee)*   *(mah-gah-dee-mahss)*   *(mēh-toh-doo)* *(mahss-soo-goo)* *(ee-kee-mahss)* *(soh-deh)* *(kah-dah)*
Koko o migi ni magarimasu. Go mētoru massugu ikimasu. Sore kara
here   (P) to the right   turn   five   meters   straight ahead   go   and   then

(hee-dah-dee) *(mah-gah-dee-mahss)* *(kah-doh)*   *(bee-joo-tsoo-kahn)*
hidari ni magarimasu. Kado ni bijutsukan ga arimasu.
to the left   turn   corner   on museum

Are you lost? There is no need to be lost if **anata wa** have learned the basic **hōkō no**

(hōh-kōh)
(P)   direction (P)

tango. Do not try to memorize these **kaiwa** because you will never be looking for

(kye-wah)
conversations

precisely these places. One day you might need to ask for **hōkō** to "**Ginza Resutoran**" or

(hōh-kōh) *(geen-zah)*
directions

"**Kyōto Bijutsukan**" or "**Miyako Hoteru.**" Learn the key **hōkō no tango** and be sure

(kyōh-toh) (bee-joo-tsoo-kahn) *(mee-yah-koh)*
museum   capital   direction (P) words

anata wa can find your **yukisaki. Anata wa** may want to buy a guidebook to start

(yoo-kee-sah-kee)
destination

planning what places **anata** would like to visit.

What if the **hito** responding to your **shitsumon** answers too quickly for you to

(shee-tsoo-mohn)
question

understand the entire reply? Just ask again, saying,

☐ **māketto** *(māh-ket-toh)*	market	_____
☐ **māku** *(māh-koo)*	mark, label	_____
☐ **māmarēdo** *(māh-mah-dēh-doh)*	marmalade	_____
☐ **mandorin** *(mahn-doh-deen)*	mandolin	_____
☐ **manējā** *(mah-nēh-jāh)*	manager	_____

(shee-tsoo-day)   *(wah-tah-shee)*   *(ah-meh-dee-kah-jeen)*   *(soo-koh-shee)(hah-nah-shee-mahss)*

Shitsurei desu ga watashi wa Amerikajin desu. Nihongo o sukoshi hanashimasu.
excuse me   but   I   American   am   little   speak

(moht-toh) *(yook-koo-dee)* *(hah-nah-shee-mahss)*   *(ee-chee-doh)*   *(ah-dee-gah-tōh)* *(goh-zye-mahss)*

Motto yukkuri hanashimasu. Mō ichido kudasai. Arigatō gozaimasu.
more   slowly   speak   once more   thank you

(eh)
Ee, it is difficult at first but don't give up! Now when the **hōkō** are repeated, **anata wa**
yes   directions

will be able to understand if **anata wa** have learned the key **hōkō no tango.** Quiz yourself
                                                           (P)

(tah-dah-shēē)
by filling in the blanks **shita** with the **tadashii Nihongo no tango.**
                             correct   (P)

Akira: *(shee-tsoo-day)*   *(fah-mee-dee)*
Shitsurei desu ga Famiri Resutoran wa doko desu ka?
       excuse me   but   family

Yoko: **Koko** *(kah-dah)* **kara** _____ *(ee-kee-mahss)* **ikimasu.** **Sore kara** *(sahn-bahn-meh)* **sanbanme** *(mee-chee)(deh)* **no michi de**
     here   from   (straight ahead)   go   third   (P)   street   at

                _____ *(mah-gah-dee-mahss)* **magarimasu.** **Soko ni** *(kyōh-kai)* **kyōkai ga arimasu.** **Kyōkai de**
                        (to the right)   turn   there   church   at

                _____ *(mah-gah-dee-mahss)* **magarimasu.** *(kah-doh)* **Kado ni Famiri Resutoran ga arimasu.**
                        (to the left)   turn   corner

Yukio: *(shee-tsoo-day)*   *(mee-yah-koh)*
Shitsurei desu ga Miyako Hoteru wa doko desu ka?
       excuse me   but   capital

Fusaka: *(nee-bahn-meh)*   *(mee-chee)*
Nibanme no michi no _____ **desu.**
      second   (P)   street   (P)   (on the left)

(moht-toh) *(ah-tah-dah-shēē)*
Koko ni motto atarashii dōshi ga arimasu.
        more   new

(maht-teh)(ee-mahss)
matte imasu = wait for   *matte imasu* _____

(wah-kah-dee-mahss)
wakarimasu = understand _____

(oo-dee-mahss)
urimasu = sell _____

(koo-dee-kah-eh-shee-mahss)
kurikaeshimasu = repeat _____

☐ **manekin** *(mah-neh-keen)* . . . . mannequin   _____
☐ **marason** *(mah-dah-sohn)* . . . . marathon   _____
☐ **maruku** *(mah-doo-koo)* . . . . mark   _____
☐ **masāji** *(mah-sāh-jee)* . . . . massage   _____
☐ **masukotto** *(mah-soo-koht-toh)* . . . . mascot   _____

As always, say each sentence out loud. Say each and every **tango** carefully, pronouncing

each **Nihongo** sound as well as **anata** can.
Japanese

(maht-teh) (ee-mahss)
matte imasu
wait for
(den-shah)
Watashi wa densha o _____ .
(P)   train   (P)

(bah-soo)
Kare   **wa basu o** _____ .
Kanojo   bus

(tah-koo-shee)
Anata wa takushii o _____ .
taxi

(hoh-teh-doo)
Watashitachi wa hoteru no naka de _____ .
hotel   (P)   inside

(dess-toh-dahn)
Karera wa resutoran no naka de _____ .
restaurant   (P)

(oo-dee-mahss)
urimasu
sell
(hah-nah)
Watashi wa hana o _____ .
flowers (P)

(koo-dah-moh-noh)
Kare   **wa kudamono o** _____ .
Kanojo   fruit

(jah-keh-tsoo)
Anata wa jaketsu o *urimasu* .
jacket

(bah-nah-nah)
Watashitachi wa banana o _____ .
bananas

(keep-poo)
Karera wa kippu o _____ .
tickets

(wah-kah-dee-mahss)
wakarimasu
understand
(ay-goh)
Watashi wa Eigo ga _____ .
(P)

(nee-hohn-goh)
Kare   **wa Nihongo ga** _____ .
Kanojo

(foo-dahn-soo-goh)
Anata wa Furansugo ga _____ .
French

(men-yoo)
Watashitachi wa menyū ga _____ .
menu

(doh-shee-ah-goh)
Karera wa Roshiago ga _____ .
Russian

(koo-dee-kah-eh-shee-mahss)
kurikaeshimasu
repeat
Watashi wa tango o _____ .

(koh-tah-eh)
Kare   **wa kotae o** _____ .
Kanojo   answer

(nah-mah-eh)
Anata wa namae o _____ .
names

(hōh-kōh)
Watashitachi wa hōkō o _____ .
directions

Karera wa bangō o _____ .

(shtah)
Ima see if **anata wa** can translate the following thoughts into **Nihongo**. **Kotae wa shita**
below

(ah-dee-mahss)
ni arimasu.
are

1. She repeats the word. _____
2. You sell tickets. _____
3. He waits for the taxi. _____
4. We eat fruit. _____
5. They understand Japanese. _____
6. I drink tea. _____

52

(oo-eh) *(shtah)*
Ue, Shita
above   below

Before **anata wa** begin Step 14, review Step 8. *(ee-mah)* *(moht-toh)* *(ah-tah-dah-shēē)*
Ima wa motto atarashii tango o
now   more   new   (P)

(nah-die-mahss)
naraimasu.
we learn

(koh-deh) *(ee-eh)*
Kore ga Nihon no ie desu.
this   (P)   (P) house

(sheen-shee-tsoo) *(oo-eh)*
Shinshitsu wa ue desu.
bedroom   above

(foo-doh-bāh) *(oo-eh)*
Furobā mo ue desu.
bathroom also above

(ee-mah) *(shtah)*
Ima wa shita desu.
living room below

(shoh-sigh) *(shtah)*
Shosai mo shita desu.
study   below

Ima go to your **shinshitsu** and look around the **heya.** Let's learn the **namae** of the **mono**
(sheen-shee-tsoo) bedroom *(heh-yah)* room *(nah-mah-eh)* names *(moh-noh)* things

in the **shinshitsu,** just like **watashitachi** learned the various parts of the **ie.** Be sure to
(ee-eh) house

practice saying the **tango** as **anata** write them in the spaces **shita.** Also say out loud the
(shtah) below

example sentences under the **e.**
(eh) pictures

(bed-doh)
beddo
bed

(kah-keh-boo-tohn)
kakebuton
quilt

(mah-koo-dah)
makura
pillow

kakebuton

(bed-doh)
Beddo o kaimasu.
bed

(kah-keh-boo-tohn) *(ee-dee-mahss)*
Kakebuton ga irimasu.
quilt   (P) I need

(mah-koo-dah) *(ōh-kēē)*
Makura wa ōkii desu.
pillow   big

☐ **masuku** *(mah-soo-koo)* .... mask, respirator
☐ **masuto** *(mah-soo-toh)* .... mast
☐ **matchi** *(maht-chee)* .... match, box of matches
☐ **mattoresu** *(maht-toh-deh-soo)* .... mattress
☐ **mayonēzu** *(mah-yoh-nēh-zoo)* .... mayonnaise

53

(meh-zah-mah-shee) (doh-kay)
mezamashi dokei
alarm   clock

(yōh-foo-koo) (dahn-soo)
yōfuku dansu
clothes   closet

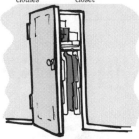

If **anata wa** have trouble understanding sentences in **Nihongo**, DON'T PANIC. Just translate them backwards!

(ee-mah)
Ima remove the next **go mai no**
now   five   (M)   (P)

(moh-noh)
stickers and label these **mono** in
                                  things

(sheen-shee-tsoo)
your **shinshitsu.**
    bedroom

(meh-zah-mah-shee)(doh-kay)
Mezamashi dokei o
alarm   clock
(moht-teh) (ee-mahss)
motte imasu.
I have

(sheen-shee-tsoo)
Shinshitsu ni wa
bedroom   in
(yōh-foo-koo) (dahn-soo)
yōfuku dansu ga
clothes   closet
(ah-dee-mahss)
arimasu.
there is

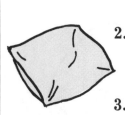

(ee-eh)   *(sheen-shee-tsoo)*
Nihon no ie no naka no shinshitsu.
      (P)   house   inside   (P)   bedroom

shin = to bed, **shitsu** = room,

so a bedroom

(shee-tsoo-mohn)
Study the following **shitsumon** and
                            questions

(koh-tah-eh)   *(hee-dah-dee)* *(eh)*
their **kotae** based on the **hidari no e.**
    answers   left   (P)   picture

(meh-zah-mah-shee) (doh-kay)   *(doh-koh)*
1. **Mezamashi dokei wa doko desu ka?**
    alarm   clock   where   is
                    (tēh-boo-doo) *(oo-eh)*
    Mezamashi dokei wa tēburu no ue desu.
                        table   top

(kah-keh-boo-tohn) (toh) (mah-koo-dah)
2. **Kakebuton to makura wa doko desu ka?**
    quilt   and   pillow
                         (bed-doh) *(oo-eh)*
    Kakebuton to makura wa beddo no ue desu.
                          bed   top   on

(yōh-foo-koo) (dahn-soo) (toh)
3. **Yōfuku dansu to beddo wa doko desu ka?**
    clothes   closet   and
              (toh)   *(sheen-shee-tsoo)* *(nah-kah)*
    Yōfuku dansu to beddo wa shinshitsu no naka desu.
                  and   bedroom   inside

            (ōh-kēē)   *(ah-doo-ee)* *(chēē-sigh)*
4. **Beddo wa ōkii desu ka, arui wa chiisai desu ka?**
           big   is   or   (P)   small
           (chēē-sigh)
    Beddo wa chiisai desu.
        (P)   small

☐ **medaru** *(meh-dah-doo)* .... medal
☐ **mēdo** *(mēh-doh)* .... maid
☐ **megahon** *(meh-gah-hohn)* .... megaphone
☐ **memo** *(meh-moh)* .... memo, memorandum
☐ **meriigōraundo** *(meh-dee-gōh-down-doh)* . merry-go-round

Ima anata wa answer the *(shee-tsoo-mohn)* **shitsumon** based on the previous *(eh)* **e**.
questions

(meh-zah-mah-shee) *(doh-kay)*
Mezamashi dokei wa doko desu ka?
alarm   clock

(bed-doh)
Beddo wa doko desu ka?
bed

_____

Beddo wa

Let's move into the *(foo-doh-bāh)* **furobā** and do the same thing.

(sen-men-die)
senmendai
washstand

(shah-wāh)
shawā
shower

(toy-deh)
toire
toilet

senmendai

_____

_____

(hoh-teh-doo) *(heh-yah)* *(nee)*
Hoteru no heya ni wa
hotel   (P)   room   in

(sen-men-die) *(ah-dee-mahss)*
senmendai ga arimasu.
washstand   there is

(heh-yah)
Hoteru no heya ni wa
(P)   room

(shah-wāh)
shawā ga arimasu.
shower   there is

(toy-deh)
Hoteru no heya ni wa toire
(P)   toilet

(dyoh-kahn)
ga arimasu. Ryokan no shawā
inn   (P)

(toh) *(beh-tsoo)*
to toire wa betsu no heya desu.
and   separate (P) rooms

(kah-gah-mee)
kagami _____
mirror

(tah-oh-doo)
taoru _____
towels

(teh-noo-goo-ee)
tenugui _____
handtowel

(yoo-ah-gah-dee) *(tah-oh-doo)*
yuagari taoru _____
bathtowel

(toh) *(dyoh-kahn)* *(deh)*
Nihon no hoteru to ryokan de, anata wa will also be given a
(P)   and inns   at

(yoo-kah-tah) *(oh-foo-doh)*
yukata to wear after your **ofuro**.
cotton robe   bath

(nah-nah) *(foo-doh-bāh)*
Do not forget to remove the next **nana mai no** stickers and label these **mono** in your **furobā**.
seven (M) (P)   bathroom

55

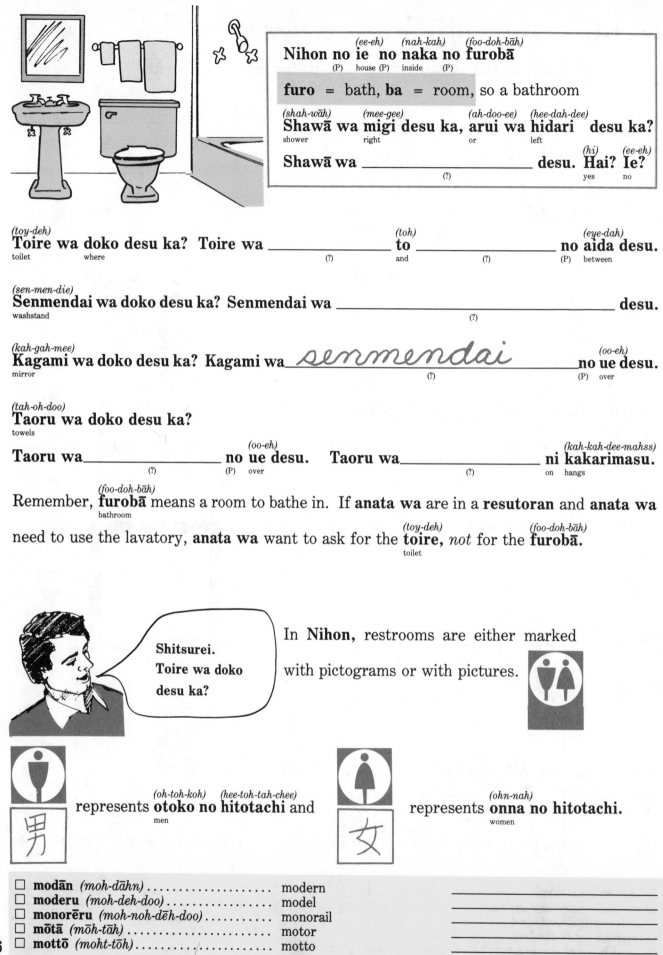

(ee-eh) (nah-kah) (foo-doh-bāh)
Nihon no ie no naka no furobā
(P) house (P) inside (P)

furo = bath, **ba** = room, so a bathroom

(shah-wāh) (mee-gee) (ah-doo-ee) (hee-dah-dee)
Shawā wa migi desu ka, arui wa hidari desu ka?
shower right or left

(hi) (ee-eh)
Shawā wa _____ **desu. Hai? Ie?**
(?) yes no

(toy-deh) (toh) (eye-dah)
Toire wa doko desu ka? Toire wa _____ **to** _____ **no aida desu.**
toilet where (?) and (?) (P) between

(sen-men-die)
Senmendai wa doko desu ka? Senmendai wa _____ **desu.**
washstand (?)

(kah-gah-mee) (oo-eh)
Kagami wa doko desu ka? Kagami wa _*senmendai*_____ **no ue desu.**
mirror (?) (P) over

(tah-oh-doo)
Taoru wa doko desu ka?
towels

(oo-eh) (kah-kah-dee-mahss)
Taoru wa _____ **no ue desu. Taoru wa** _____ **ni kakarimasu.**
(?) (P) over (?) on hangs

(foo-doh-bāh)
Remember, **furobā** means a room to bathe in. If **anata wa** are in a **resutoran** and **anata wa**
bathroom

(toy-deh) (foo-doh-bāh)
need to use the lavatory, **anata wa** want to ask for the **toire**, *not* for the **furobā**.
toilet

Shitsurei.
Toire wa doko
desu ka?

In **Nihon**, restrooms are either marked
with pictograms or with pictures.

男 represents **otoko no hitotachi** and
(oh-toh-koh) (hee-toh-tah-chee)
men

女 represents **onna no hitotachi.**
(ohn-nah)
women

☐ **modān** (moh-dāhn) .... modern
☐ **moderu** (moh-deh-doo) .... model
☐ **monorēru** (moh-noh-dēh-doo) .... monorail
☐ **mōtā** (mōh-tāh) .... motor
☐ **motto** (moht-tōh) ..../...... motto

Next stop — the **shosai**, specifically the **tēburu** or the **tsukue** in the
(shoh-sigh) study   *(tēh-boo-doo)* table   *(tsoo-koo-eh)* desk

(shoh-sigh) *(tsoo-koo-eh)* *(oo-eh)* *(nah-nee)*
shosai. Tsukue no ue ni nani ga arimasu ka? Let's identify the **mono** that one normally
desk   desk   (P) top on what   is there

(tsoo-koo-eh)
finds on the **tsukue** or strewn about the **ie.**
desk

(en-pee-tsoo)
enpitsu
pencil

(pen)
pen
pen

(kah-mee)
kami
paper

(teh-gah-mee)
tegami
letter

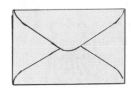

_____

(hah-gah-kee)
hagaki
postcard

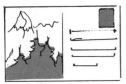

(keet-teh)
kitte
stamp

kitte

(hohn)
hon
book

(zahsh-shee)
zasshi
magazine

THE JAPAN TIMES

_____

(sheen-boon)
shinbun
newspaper

ASAHI WEEKLY

(meh-gah-neh)
megane
eyeglasses

(teh-deh-bee-jone) *(teh-deh-bee)*
terebijon /**terebi**
television   t.v.

(goh-mee-bah-koh)
gomibako
wastepaper basket

_____

☐ **naifu** *(nye-foo)* .... knife	_____
☐ **napukin** *(nah-poo-keen)* .... napkin	_____
☐ **natto** *(naht-toh)* .... nut	_____
☐ **nekkachiifu** *(nek-kah-chēē-foo)* .... neckerchief	_____
☐ **nekkuresu** *(nek-koo-deh-soo)* .... necklace	_____

57

Ima label these **mono** in your **shosai** *(shoh-sigh)* study with your stickers. Do not forget to say these **tango** out loud whenever **anata wa** write them, **anata wa** see them or **anata wa** apply the stickers. **Ima** identify the **mono** in the **e no shita** *(eh)* *(shtah)* (P) below by filling in each blank with the **tadashii** *(tah-dah-shēē)* correct **Nihongo no tango.** (P)

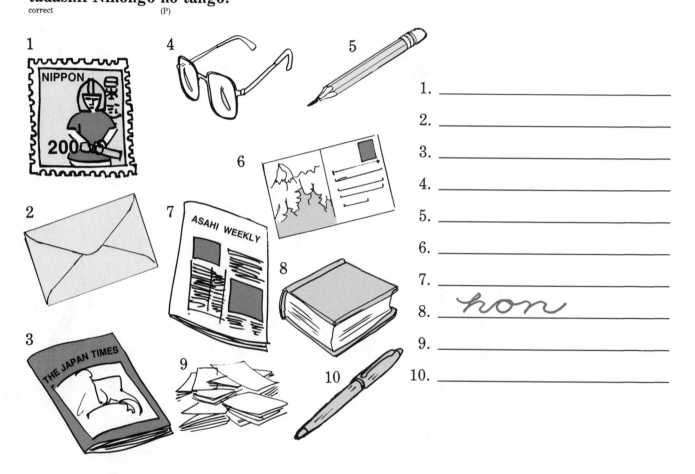

1. NIPPON 200
2.
3. THE JAPAN TIMES
4.
5.
6.
7. ASAHI WEEKLY
8.
9.
10.

1. _____
2. _____
3. _____
4. _____
5. _____
6. _____
7. _____
8. *hon*
9. _____
10. _____

Koko ni motto atarashii dōshi ga arimasu. *(moht-toh)* *(ah-tah-dah-shēē)* more new

mimasu *(mee-mahss)* = see	**okurimasu** *(oh-koo-dee-mahss)* = send	**nemasu** *(neh-mahss)* = sleep	**sagashimasu** *(sah-gah-shee-mahss)* = look for

mimasu _____ _____ _____

Ima fill in the blanks, on the **tsugi no pēji,** *(tsoo-gee)* following (P) with the **tadashii** *(tah-dah-shēē)* correct form of these **dōshi.**

Practice saying the sentences out loud many times.

☐ **nekutai** *(neh-koo-tie)* .... necktie _____
☐ **neon** *(neh-ohn)* .... neon _____
☐ **netto** *(net-toh)* .... net _____
☐ **nōto** *(nōh-toh)* .... note _____
☐ **nyūsu** *(nyōō-soo)* .... news _____

58

(mee-mahss)
mimasu
see

Watashi wa beddo ga *(bed-doh)* *(gah)* _mimasu_ .
bed (P)

Kare wa kakebuton ga *(kah-keh-boo-tohn)* _____ .
Kanojo quilt

Anata wa hoteru ga *(hoh-teh-doo)* _____ .
hotel

Watashitachi wa Fujisan ga *(foo-jee-sahn)* _____ .
Mt. Fuji

Karera wa ie ga *(ee-eh)* _____ .
house

(oh-koo-dee-mahss)
okurimasu
send

Watashi wa tegami o *(teh-gah-mee)* *(oh)* _____ .
letter (P)

Kare wa hagaki o *(hah-gah-kee)* _____ .
Kanojo postcard

Anata wa hon o *(hohn)* _____ .
book

Watashitachi wa shinbun o *(sheen-boon)* _____ .
newspaper

Karera wa zasshi o *(zahsh-shee)* _____ .
magazine

(neh-mahss)
nemasu
sleep

Watashi wa shinshitsu de *(sheen-shee-tsoo)* *(deh)* _____ .
bedroom in

Kare wa beddo de *(deh)* _nemasu_ .
Kanojo in

Anata wa hoteru de *(hoh-teh-doo)* _____ .
hotel

Watashitachi wa ie de *(ee-eh)* _____ .
house

Karera wa ryokan de *(dyoh-kahn)* _____ .
inn

(sah-gah-shee-mahss)
sagashimasu
look for

Watashi wa kitte o *(keet-teh)* *(oh)* _____ .
stamp (P)

Kare wa shinbun o *(sheen-boon)* _____ .
Kanojo newspaper

Anata wa megane o *(meh-gah-neh)* _____ .
eyeglasses

Watashitachi wa ryokan o *(dyoh-kahn)* _____ .
inn

Karera wa hana o *(hah-nah)* _____ .
flowers

Terms of respect, such as "*(oh)* **o**" and "*(sahn)* **san**" are **hijō** *(hee-jōh)* **ni taisetsu** *(tie-seh-tsoo)* in **Nihongo**. "O,"
very important

meaning "honorable," is normally added to the beginning of **tango:**

o + cha =	**ocha,** *(oh-chah)*	
	tea	"honorable" tea
o + hashi =	**ohashi.** *(oh-hah-shee)*	
	chopsticks	"honorable" chopsticks

"**San,**" which means "Mr.," "Mrs.," "Miss" or "honorable," is added to the end of **tango**

or to **hito no namae:** *(hee-toh)*
person (P)

oba + san =	**obasan,** *(oh-bah-sahn)*
aunt	honorable aunt
Tanaka + san =	**Tanakasan.** *(tah-nah-kah-sahn)*
	Mr. Tanaka

Step 15

(yōo-bean)
Yūbin
mail

(ah-nah-tah)
Anata wa know how to count, how to ask **shitsumon,** how to use **dōshi** with the "plug-in"
you (P)   *(shee-tsoo-mohn)* questions   *(dōh-shee)* verbs

formula, how to make statements, and how to describe **mono,** be it the location of a

(ah-doo-ee) *(ee-eh)* *(ee-doh)*
hoteru, arui wa ie no iro. Ima take the basics that **anata wa** have learned and expand
or   house (P) color

them in special areas that will be most helpful in your travels. **Nani** does everyone do on
(nah-nee) what

(hah-gah-kee)
a holiday? Send **hagaki,** of course! Let's learn exactly how the **Nihon no yūbinkyoku**
postcards   (P)   *(yōo-bean-kyoh-koo)* post office

works.

(yōo-bean)
yūbin . . .
mail

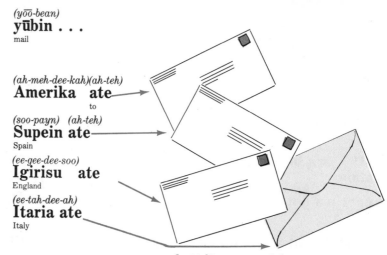

(ah-meh-dee-kah)(ah-teh)
Amerika ate
to

(soo-payn) (ah-teh)
Supein ate
Spain

(ee-gee-dee-soo)
Igirisu ate
England

(ee-tah-dee-ah)
Itaria ate
Italy

(yōo-bean-kyoh-koo)
Yūbinkyoku is where **anata wa** need to go in **Nihon** to buy a **kitte,** mail a **kozutsumi,**
post office   *(keet-teh)* stamp   *(koh-zoo-tsoo-mee)* package

(den-pōh)   *(den-wah)*   *(yōo-bean-kyoh-koo)*
send a **denpō** or use the **denwa. Koko ni** are some necessary **tango** for the **yūbinkyoku**
telegram   telephone   post office

Be sure to practice them out loud and then write the **tango** below the **e.**
(eh)

(teh-gah-mee)
tegami
letter

(hah-gah-kee)
hagaki
postcard

(keet-teh)
kitte
stamp

(den-pōh)
denpō
telegram

NIPPON
200

DENPŌ

——————   ——————   ——————   *denpō*

☐ **ōpun** *(ōh-poon)* . . . . open
☐ **orenji** *(oh-den-jee)* . . . . orange
☐ **orugan** *(oh-doo-gahn)* . . . . organ
☐ **ōtobai** *(ōh-toh-by)* . . . . motorbike
60 ☐ **ōtomiiru** *(ōh-toh-mēe-doo)* . . . . oatmeal

(koh-zoo-tsoo-mee)
kozutsumi
package

(yōo-bean-bah-koh)
yūbinbako
mailbox

(kōh-kōo-bean)
kōkūbin
airmail

KŌKŪBIN
AIRMAIL

(oo-keh-tsoo-keh)
uketsuke
counter/front desk

_____   _____   _____

(den-wah) *(bohk-soo)*
denwa bokusu
telephone   booth

(den-wah)
denwa
telephone

(yōo-bean-kyoh-koo)
yūbinkyoku
post office

denwa

_____   _____   _____

Nihon no *(yōo-bean-kyoh-koo)* **yūbinkyoku ni wa** *(zen-boo)* **zenbu ga arimasu.** *(yōo-bean-kyoh-koo)* **Yūbinkyoku kara wa** *(hah-gah-kee)(teh-gah-mee)* **hagaki, tegami,**
(P)   in   everything   there is   from   postcards

(toh) *(den-pōh)* **to denpō o** *(oh-koo-deh-mahss)* **okurimasu. Yūbinkyoku de** *(keet-teh)* **kitte o** *(kye-mahss)* **kaimasu. Yūbinkyoku kara denwa o**
and telegrams   send   at   stamps   buy

(kah-keh-mahss) **kakemasu. Yūbinkyoku is open from kuji to goji on** *(hay-jee-tsoo)* **heijitsu and from kuji to** *(jōo-nee-jee)* **jūniji**
call   nine o'clock   five o'clock   weekdays   half past 12

(hahn) *(doh-yōh-bee)* **han on Doyōbi. Yūbinkyoku is closed on** *(kyōo-kah)* **kyūka and** *(nee-chee-yōh-bee)* **Nichiyōbi. In Nihon, anata wa can**
Saturdays   holidays   Sundays

also obtain postal supplies at your hoteru no uketsuke.
(P)   front desk

Okay. First step — enter the *(yōo-bean-kyoh-koo)* **yūbinkyoku.**
post office

The following is a good sample *(kye-wah)* **kaiwa. Familiarize yourself with kono tango now.**
conversation   these

Shitsurei desu ga kitte wa doko de kaemasu ka?

(bahn)
Nana ban no
number
uketsuke.

NANA BAN

□ **okesutora** *(oh-keh-soo-toh-dah)* . . . . orchestra
□ **omuretsu** *(oh-moo-deh-tsoo)* . . . . omelette
□ **ōnā** *(ōh-nāh)* . . . . owner
□ **onsu** *(ohn-soo)* . . . . ounce
□ **opera** *(oh-peh-dah)* . . . . opera

 Tegami to hagaki no kitte o kudasai.

 Kōkūbin?

 Ikura desu ka?

 Tegami ga nihyaku yonjū en (¥ 240), hagaki ga hyaku jū en (¥ 110).

 Kōkūbin o kudasai. Sore kara Nihon no kitte o kudasai. Ikura desu ka?

 Nihyaku sanjū en (¥ 230).

(hi)
Hai. Kekko desu.
yes   fine

Kore ga kitte desu. Gohyaku hachijū en (¥ 580).

(dōh-moh)
Dōmo.
thanks

Next step — **anata wa** ask **shitsumon** *(shee-tsoo-mohn)* like those **shita**, *(shtah)* depending on what **anata wa** **irimasu.** *(ee-dee-mahss)*

questions (below) (below) (need)

(keet-teh) *(kye-mahss)*
Kitte wa doko de kaimasu ka?
stamps   where at buy

(hah-gah-kee)
Hagaki wa doko de kaimasu ka?
postcards

(den-wah) *(bohk-soo)*
Denwa bokusu wa doko desu ka?
telephone booth

(kōh-shōō)
Kōshū denwa wa doko desu ka?
public

(yōō-bean-bah-koh)
Yūbinbako wa doko desu ka?
mailbox

(den-pōh) *(oh-koo-dee-mahss)*
Denpō wa doko kara okurimasu ka?
telegram   from   send

(koh-zoo-tsoo-mee)
Kozutsumi wa doko kara okurimasu ka?
package

(ee-koo-dah)
Kitte wa ikura desu ka?
          how much

Hagaki wa ikura desu ka?

(soh-deh)
Sore wa ikura desu ka?
that

Practice these sentences again and again.

Ima quiz yourself. See if **anata wa** can translate the following thoughts into **Nihongo.**

Kotae wa tsugi no pēji no shita ni arimasu. *(tsoo-gee)*
next   (P)   (P)

1. Where is a telephone booth? _____

2. Where is a mailbox? *Yūbinbako wa doko desu ka?*

3. Where is a public telephone? _____

4. Where is the post office? _____

5. Where do I buy postcards? _____

☐ **pai** *(pie)* . . . . pie
☐ **painappuru** *(pie-nahp-poo-doo)* . . . . pineapple
☐ **paipu** *(pie-poo)* . . . . pipe
☐ **pajama** *(pah-jah-mah)* . . . . pajamas
☐ **pakkingu** *(pahk-keen-goo)* . . . . packing

6. Where do I buy stamps? _____

7. Airmail stamps? _____

8. Where do I send a package? _____

9. Where do I send a telegram? _____

10. Where is the front desk? _____

Koko ni motto atarashii dōshi ga arimasu.
(moht-toh) (ah-tah-dah-shēē)
here   more   new   verbs

(shee-mahss)
shimasu = do   *(kah-kee-mahss)* **kakimasu** = write   *(mee-seh-mahss)* **misemasu** = show   *(hah-die-mahss)* **haraimasu** = pay

_____ *kakimasu* _____

(shee-mahss)
shimasu
do

Watashi wa shigoto o _____ .
(shee-goh-toh)   work

Kare   wa sukoshi _____ .
Kanojo   *(soo-koh-shee)* a little

Anata wa takusan *skimasu* .
(tah-koo-sahn)   a lot

Watashitachi wa kyō _____ .
(kyōh) today

Karera wa zenbu _____ .
(zen-boo) everything

(mee-seh-mahss)
misemasu
show

Watashi wa kare ni hon o _____ .
(kah-deh)   him   (P)

Kare   wa anata ni tsukue o _____ .
Kanojo   *(tsoo-koo-eh)*   desk

Anata wa kare ni ryokan o _____ .
(dyoh-kahn) inn

Watashitachi wa kare ni terebi o _____ .
(teh-deh-bee) t.v.

Karera wa kare ni hoteru o _____ .

(kah-kee-mahss)
kakimasu
write

Watashi wa tegami o *kakimasu* .
(teh-gah-mee) letter

Kare   wa sukoshi _____ .
Kanojo   *(soo-koh-shee)* a little

Anata wa sain o _____ .
(sign) signature

Watashitachi wa denpō o _____ .
(den-pōh) telegram

Karera wa hagaki _____ .
(hah-gah-kee) postcards

(hah-die-mahss)
haraimasu
pay

Watashi wa kanjōgaki o _____ .
(kahn-jōh-gah-kee) bill

Kare   wa zeikin o _____ .
Kanojo   *(zay-keen)* tax

Anata wa zenbu _____ .
(zen-boo) everything

Watashitachi wa nedan o _____ .
(neh-dahn) price

Karera wa ryokin *haraimasu* .
(dyoh-keen) fare

KOTAE

1. Denwa bokusu wa doko desu ka?
2. Yūbinbako wa doko desu ka?
3. Kōshū denwa wa doko desu ka?
4. Yūbinkyoku wa doko desu ka?
5. Hagaki wa doko de kaemasu ka?

6. Kitte wa doko de kaemasu ka?
7. Kōkūbin kitte?
8. Kozutsumi wa doko kara okurimasu ka?
9. Denpō wa doko kara okurimasu ka?
10. Uketsuke wa doko desu ka?

63

Step 16

(kahn-jōh-gah-kee) *(dyōh-shōō-shoh)*

Kanjōgaki arui wa Ryōshūsho

(eh)
Ee, there are also **kanjōgaki** to pay in **Nihon.** **Anata wa** have just finished your evening
yes   *(kahn-jōh-gah-kee)*
bills

meal and **anata wa** would like to pay your **kanjōgaki.** **Dō** do **anata wa** go about this?
(kahn-jōh-gah-kee) *(dōh)*
bill   how

Anata wa call your **uētā** **arui wa** **uētoresu** and say, "Kanjōgaki o kudasai."
(ōō-eh-tāh) *(ah-doo-ee)* *(oo-ēh-toh-deh-soo)*
waiter   or   waitress

Kanjōgaki o kudasai.

(oo-ēh-tāh)
The **uētā** will normally reel off what **anata wa**
waiter

have eaten, while writing rapidly. Then the
(oo-ēh-tāh) *(ee-chee)* *(my)* *(kah-mee)*
uētā will give you **ichi** **mai** **no** **kami** that
one sheet (P) paper
(eh)

looks like the **kanjōgaki** in the **e,** while

saying something like

(gōh-kay) *(hyah-koo)*
"Gōkei de sen ni hyaku en desu."
total   of   1,000 + 200 = 1,200

(oo-keh-tsoo-keh)
Then **anata wa** take your **kanjōgaki** to the **uketsuke** to pay the cashier. **Anata wa** can
counter

(oo-ēh-tāh)
also give the **uētā** **okane** and **kanjōgaki.** **Kare** will then bring **anata** your change.
waiter money

(cheep-poo)
Remember that in **Nihon** it is not customary to leave a **chippu** because a service charge is
tip

(gōh-kay)
already included in the **gōkei** on the **kanjōgaki.**
total

(dōh-moh)(ah-dee-gah-tōh)
"Dōmo arigatō
thank you very much
(goh-zye-mahss)
gozaimasu."

(goh-chee-sōh-sah-mah)
"Gochisōsama."
delicious

Anata wa will notice that refills of **ocha** are

not included on the **kanjōgaki.** In **Nihon,**
(kohp-poo)
your **koppu** will be gladly filled time and time
cup

again at no extra charge. After **anata wa**

have paid the **kanjōgaki,** the **uētā** or cashier
(mah-tah) *(dōh-zoh)*
will very likely say "Mata dōzo," which

means "Please come again."

□ **pankēki** *(pahn-kēh-kee)* .... pancake   _____
□ **panku** *(pahn-koo)* .... puncture   _____
□ **panorama** *(pah-noh-dah-mah)* .... panorama   _____
□ **pantsu** *(pahn-tsoo)* .... pants   _____
64 □ **papaia** *(pah-pie-ah)* .... papaya   _____

Remember these key **tango** when dining out in **Nihon**.

(men-yōō) **menyū**	(kahn-jōh-gah-kee) **kanjōgaki**	(oo-ēh-tāh) **uētā**	(oo-ēh-toh-deh-soo) **uētoresu**
menu	bill	waiter	waitress

Politeness is **hijō ni taisetsu** *(tie-seh-tsoo)* in Nihon. **Anata wa** will feel more **Nihon teki** *(teh-kee)* if **anata**
important   Japanese   like

practice and use **tsugi no hyōgen.** **kudasai** *(koo-dah-sigh)*   **sumimasen** *(soo-mee-mah-sen)*
(tsoo-gee) *(hyōh-gen)*   please/please give me   sorry (to bother you)
following (P) expressions

shitsurei *(shee-tsoo-day)*   **arigatō gozaimasu** *(ah-dee-gah-tōh)(goh-zye-mahss)*   **dōmo** *(dōh-moh)*   **dō itashimashite** *(dōh)* *(ee-tah-shee-mah-shtay)*
excuse me   thank you   thanks   you're welcome

Koko ni is a sample **kaiwa** *(kye-wah)* involving paying the **kanjōgaki** *(kahn-jōh-gah-kee)* when leaving a **hoteru**.
                                  conversation   bill

Tanakasan:	**Sumimasen. Kanjōgaki o kudasai.** *(soo-mee-mah-sen)*
	sorry to bother you bill
Manējā: *(mah-nēh-jāh)*	**Heya wa nan ban desu ka?** *(heh-yah)*
manager	room what number
Tanakasan:	**Yonhyakujū ban desu.** *(yohn-hyah-koo-jōō)*
Manējā:	**Dōmo. Chotto matte kudasai.** *(dōh-moh)* *(choht-toh)* *(maht-teh)*
	thanks just a minute wait
	Kanjōgaki wa ichiman nisen en desu.
	10,000 + 2,000 = 12,000
Tanakasan:	**Dōmo.** (Tanakasan hands the **manējā ichiman en to gosen en satsu.**
	10,000 and 5,000 bills
	Manējā returns shortly and **iimasu)** *(ēē-mahss)*
	says
Manējā:	**Kore ga ryōshūsho to otsuri desu. Arigatō gozaimasu. Sayonara.** *(dyōh-shōō-shoh)* *(toh)* *(oh-tsoo-dee)* *(ah-dee-gah-tōh)* *(goh-zye-mahss)* *(sigh-yoh-nah-dah)*
	this receipt and change thank you goodbye

Simple, right? If **anata wa** have any **mondai** *(mohn-die)* with **bangō,** just ask someone to write them
                                        problem

out, so that **anata** can be sure **anata wa wakarimasu** *(wah-kah-dee-mahss)* everything correctly.
                                                            understand

Bangō o kaite kudasai. Arigatō gozaimasu. *(kye-teh)*
                   write

Let's take a break from **okane** and, starting on the **tsugi no pēji,** *(tsoo-gee)* learn some **atarashii** *(ah-tah-dah-shēē)*
                         money   next   (P)   new

fun **tango.**

☐ **pārā** *(pāh-dāh)* . . . . parlor _____
☐ **parashūto** *(pah-dah-shōō-toh)* . . . . parachute _____
☐ **parasoru** *(pah-dah-soh-doo)* . . . . parasol _____
☐ **pāsento** *(pāh-sen-toh)* . . . . percent _____
☐ **paseri** *(pah-seh-dee)* . . . . parsley _____

(kah-deh) *(ken-kōh)*
Kare wa kenkō desu. Kare wa byōki desu.
he   healthy   *(byōh-kee)* sick

(soh-deh) *(ēē)*
Sore wa ii desu.
that   good

(wah-doo-ee)
Sore wa warui desu.
bad

(mee-zoo) *(ah-tsee)*
Mizu wa atsui desu.
water   hot
(doh)
Sanjūgo do desu.
35   degrees

Mizu wa tsumetai desu.
             (tsoo-meh-tie) cold

Go do desu.
five

35° C

5°C

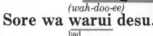

SHIZUKA NI

YAKAMASHIKU

(shee-zoo-kah)
Anata wa shizuka ni
               quietly
(hah-nah-shee-mahss)
hanashimasu.
speak

(yah-kah-mah-shee-koo)
Kare wa yakamashiku
             loudly

hanashimasu.

(ah-kye) *(sen)* *(mee-jee-kye)*
Akai sen wa mijikai desu.
red   line   short
(ah-oy) *(nah-guy)*
Aoi sen wa nagai desu.
blue   long

(ohn-nah) *(hee-toh)* *(say)* *(tah-kye)*
Onna no hito wa sei ga takai desu.
woman (P) person   height (P) tall
(koh-doh-moh) *(hee-koo-ee)*
Kodomo wa sei ga hikui desu.
child   short

(ah-tsee)
Akai hon wa atsui desu.
              thick
(oo-soo-ee)
Aoi hon wa usui desu.
             thin

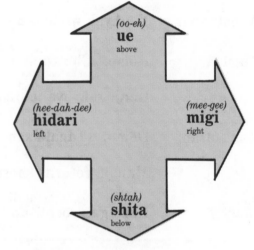

(oo-eh)
ue
above

(hee-dah-dee) *(mee-gee)*
hidari   **migi**
left   right

(shtah)
shita
below

(jee-soh-koo) *(kee-doo)*
jisoku nijū kiro
per hour   20   kilometers

(jee-soh-koo) *(kee-doo)*
jisoku nihyaku kiro
per hour   200   kilometers

(oh-soy)
osoi
slow

(hi-yi)
hayai
fast

☐ **pasu** *(pah-soo)* . . . . pass, free ticket

☐ **pasupōto** *(pah-soo-pōh-toh)* . . . . passport

☐ **pasuteru** *(pah-soo-teh-doo)* . . . . pastel

☐ **pāteii** *(pāh-teh-ēē)* . . . . party

66 ☐ **pējento** *(pēh-jen-toh)* . . . . pageant

_____

_____

_____

_____

_____

(yah-mah) *(tah-kye)* *(mēh-toh-doo)*
Yama wa takai desu. Nisen mētoru desu.
mountains high 2000 meters

(hee-koo-ee) *(nah-nah-hyah-koo)*
Yama wa hikui desu. Nanahyaku mētoru desu.
low 700

(oh-jēē-sahn) *(toh-shee-yoh-dee)* *(nah-nah-joos-sigh)*
Ojiisan wa toshiyori desu. Kare wa nanajussai desu.
grandfather old 70 years old

(koh-doh-moh) *(wah-kye)* *(taht-tah)* *(joos-sigh)*
Kodomo wa wakai desu. Kare wa tatta jussai desu.
child young only 10 years old

(tah-kye)
Hoteru wa takai desu. Niman en desu.
expensive ¥20,000

(dyoh-kahn) *(yah-soo-ee)*
Ryokan wa yasui desu. Gosen en desu.
inn inexpensive ¥5000

(moht-teh) (ee-mahss) *(kah-neh-moh-chee)* *(soh-deh)* *(tah-koo-sahn)* *(oh-kah-neh)*
Jūman en o motte imasu. Kanemochi desu. Sore wa takusan no okane desu.
¥100,000 I have rich I am that a lot (P) money

(bean-bōh) *(soo-koh-shee)*
Gohyaku en o motte imasu. Binbō desu. Sore wa sukoshi no okane desu.
¥500 poor little (P) money

Koko ni atarashii dōshi ga arimasu.
here

(sheet-teh) (ee-mahss) *(noh-dee-mahss)* *(dyoh-kōh) (shee-mahss)* *(yoh-mee-mahss)*
shitte imasu = know **norimasu** = ride **ryokō shimasu** = travel **yomimasu** = read

_____ *norimasu* _____ _____

Anata wa will use **bangō** a lot while in **Nihon.** Just remember that *(jōō)* **jū** means 10, *(hyah-koo)* **hyaku**

means 100 and **sen** means 1000. **Anata wa** will also hear *(mahn)* **man,** which means 10,000, used

frequently. To use **man** correctly, **anata wa** need to do a little arithmetic, just as

watashitachi learned in Step 6. *(tah-toh-eh-bah)* **Tatoeba,** 20,000 is *(nee-mahn)* **niman,** or **ni** (2) times **man** (10,000).
for example

Ima, how do **anata wa** say 50,000 in **Nihongo?** It's simple: **go** (5) times **man** (10,000)

(goh-mahn)
or **goman.**

☐ **pēji** *(pēh-jee)* . . . . page
☐ **pen** *(pen)* . . . . pen
☐ **penii** *(peh-nēē)* . . . . penny
☐ **pedaru** *(peh-dah-doo)* . . . . pedal
☐ **piano** *(pee-ah-noh)* . . . . piano

67

Study **kono dōshi** closely, as **anata** will use them a lot.

(sheet-teh) (ee-mahss)
shitte imasu
know

Watashi wa Eigo o _____ .

Kare
Kanojo wa anata no namae o _____ .
         your   (P)

(jōo-shoh)
Anata wa hoteru no jūsho o _____ .
         (P)   address

(soo-beh-teh)
Watashitachi wa subete _____ .
              everything

Karera wa Nihongo o _____ .

(noh-dee-mahss)
norimasu
ride

(jee-ten-shah)
Watashi wa jitensha ni _____ .
         bicycle   on

(chee-kah-teh-tsoo)
Kare
Kanojo wa chikatetsu ni _____ .
            subway

Anata wa takushii ni *norimasu* .
                in

Watashitachi wa basu ni _____ .

(jee-dōh-shah)
Karera wa jidōsha ni _____ .
              car

(dyoh-kōh) (shee-mahss)
ryokō shimasu
travel

Watashi wa Nihon ni _____ .
              to

Kare
Kanojo wa Amerika ni _____ .

Anata wa jidōsha de _____ .
              by

Watashitachi wa basu de _____ .

Karera wa densha de _____ .

(yoh-mee-mahss)
yomimasu
read

Watashi wa hon o *yomimasu* .

(zahsh-shee)
Kare
Kanojo wa zasshi o _____ .
            magazine
(men-yōo)
Anata wa menyū o _____ .
            menu

(ōh-koo)
Watashitachi wa ōku _____ .
                a lot

(sheen-boon)
Karera wa shinbun o _____ .
            newspaper

Can you translate the sentences **shita** into Nihongo? *(koh-tah-eh)* *(shtah)* **Kotae wa shita ni arimasu.**
                                                          answers   below

1. I ride the bus. *Watashi wa basu ni norimasu*

2. He reads the letter. _____

   (araimasu)
3. They wash the vegetables. _____

4. I know Japanese. _____

5. We ride in a taxi. _____

6. She knows a lot. _____

Ima draw **sen** between the opposites **shita.** Don't forget to say them out loud. Use **kono**
lines ⁽ˢʰᵗᵃʰ⁾ below

tango every day to describe the **mono** in **anata no ie,** **anata no gakkō,** at work, etc.
your ⁽ᵉᵉ⁻ᵉʰ⁾ house your ⁽ᵍᵃʰᵏ⁻ᵏᵒʰ⁾ school

(say) *(tah-kye)*
sei ga takai

(ah-tsee)
atsui

(wah-kye)
wakai

(bean-bōh)
binbō

(ken-kōh)
kenkō

(nah-guy)
nagai

(tah-koo-sahn)
takusan

(ēē)
ii

(hee-dah-dee)
hidari

(tah-kye)
takai

(ah-tsee)
atsui

(shtah)
shita

(oh-soy)
osoi

(tah-kye)
takai

(shee-zoo-kah)
shizuka ni

(oo-soo-ee)
usui

(oo-eh)
ue

(say) *(hee-koo-ee)*
sei ga hikui

(yah-kah-mah-shee-koo)
yakamashiku

(mee-jee-kye)
mijikai

(yah-soo-ee)
yasui

(hee-koo-ee)
hikui

(soo-koh-shee)
sukoshi

(byōh-kee)
byōki

(toh-shee-yoh-dee)
toshiyori

(hi-yi)
hayai

(mee-gee)
migi

(kah-neh-moh-chee)
kanemochi

(wah-doo-ee)
warui

(tsoo-meh-tie)
tsumetai

☐ **pikunikku** *(pee-koo-neek-koo)*	picnic		_____
☐ **pin** *(peen)*	pin		_____
☐ **poketto** *(poh-ket-toh)*	pocket		_____
☐ **pompu** *(pohm-poo)*	pump		_____
☐ **pondo** *(pohn-doh)*	pound		_____

69

Step 17

(dyoh-kōh) *(shee-mahss)*
Ryokō Shimasu
travel

(kee-nōh)
Kinō wa Tōkyō!
yesterday

(kyōh)
Kyō wa Kyōto!
today

(ah-shtah) *(ōh-sah-kah)*
Ashita wa Ōsaka!
tomorrow

(geh-tsoo-yōh) *(kōh-beh)*
Getsuyō wa Kōbe!
Monday

(soo-ee-yōh) *(nah-goh-yah)*
Suiyō wa Nagoya!
Wednesday

(keen-yōh) *(sahp-poh-doh)*
Kinyō wa Sapporo!
Friday

Traveling can be easy, clean and **hijō ni omoshiroi** *(hee-jōh)* *(oh-moh-shee-doy)* in **Nihon**. **Nihon** is **shimaguni** *(shee-mah-goo-nee)* and is interesting island country

roughly the size of **Kariforunia** *(kah-dee-foh-doo-nee-ah)*. There are many **ryokō no hōhō** *(dyoh-kōh)* *(hōh-hōh)* in **Nihon**.
California travel (P) ways

Tanakasan wa jidōsha de ryokō shimasu. *(jee-dōh-shah)(deh)(dyoh-kōh)* *(shee-mahss)*
Mr. Tanaka car by travels

Itosan wa hikōki de ryokō shimasu. *(hee-kōh-kee)* *(dyoh-kōh)* *(shee-mahss)*
airplane by travels

Kazuko wa densha de ryokō shimasu. *(den-shah)*
train by travels

Yoko wa fune de ryokō shimasu. *(foo-neh)*
boat by travels

Suzukisan wa jitensha de Nihon o *(jee-ten-shah)* *(nee-hohn)*
bicycle

jūdan shimasu. *(jōō-dahn)(shee-mahss)*
traverses

(hee-dah-dee) *(chee-zoo)* *(mee-teh)*
Hidari no chizu o mite
left (P) map look

kudasai. Nihon desu.

(kee-tah) *(mee-nah-mee)*
Kita kara minami made,
north from south to
(hee-kōh-kee)
hikōki de nijikan,
airplane two hours

jidōsha de gojūjikan,
50 hours

densha de jūgojikan,
15 hours
(kah-kah-dee-mahss)
kakarimasu. Nihon de no
takes (P)
(dyoh-kōh) *(ben-dee)*
ryokō wa benri desu.
travel convenient

HIKŌKI: ½ HOUR

JIDŌSHA: 10 HOURS

DENSHA 3½ HOURS

HIKŌKI: 2 HOURS

JIDŌSHA: 50 HOURS

DENSHA: 15 HOURS

☐ **posutā** *(poh-soo-tāh)* .... poster
☐ **pōtā** *(pōh-tāh)* .... porter
☐ **pudingu** *(poo-deen-goo)* .... pudding
☐ **purasu** *(poo-dah-soo)* .... plus
☐ **pūru** *(pōō-doo)* .... pool, swimming pool

70

(nee-hohn-jeen) *(yoh-koo)* *(dyoh-kōh)* *(shee-mahss)*
Nihonjin wa yoku ryokō shimasu. So it is no surprise to find many **tango** built on the
Japanese (people)   much   travel

(dyoh-kōh)
tango "ryokō" which means "journey" or "trip." Practice saying the **tsugi no tango**
                                                                                                (P)

many times. **Anata wa** will see them often.

(dyoh-kōh)
ryokō
trip, journey

(dyoh-kōh) *(shee-mahss)*
ryokō shimasu
travel

(dyoh-koh-shah)
ryokōsha
traveler/travel agency

(hee-kōh-kee) *(deh)* *(dyoh-kōh)* *(shee-mahss)*
hikōki de ryokō shimasu
airplane   by   travel

(foo-neh) *(deh)* *(dyoh-kōh)*
fune de ryokō shimasu
boat   by

(jee-dōh-shah)
jidōsha de ryokō shimasu
car   by

(den-shah)
densha de ryokō shimasu
train

(bah-soo)
basu de ryokō shimasu
bus

(jee-ten-shah)
jitensha de ryokō shimasu
bicycle

(ah-doo-ee-teh)
aruite ryokō shimasu
on foot

(dōh-zoh)(yoy) *(dyoh-kōh)*
Dōzo yoi ryokō o!
have   a good trip

(shtah)   *(sign)*
Shita ni are some basic **sain** which **anata wa** should learn to recognize quickly. Many
below   signs

(goo-chee)
of **kono tango** are based on the root **tango "guchi,"** which means "mouth" in **Nihongo.**

(ee-dee-goo-chee)
Iriguchi means "into the mouth" and *(deh-goo-chee)* **"deguchi"** means "out of the mouth."
entrance   exit

(deh-goo-chee)
deguchi _____
exit, main exit

(hee-jōh) *(deh-goo-chee)*
hijō deguchi _____
emergency exit

(ee-dee-goo-chee)
iriguchi _iriguchi_ _____
entrance

(kaht-teh-goo-chee)
katteguchi _____
side entrance

(gen-kahn)
genkan _____
main entrance

(sheen-nyōō) *(keen-shee)*
shinnyū kinshi _____
do not enter

IRIGUCHI

SHINNYŪ KINSHI

DEGUCHI

☐ **rajio** *(dah-jee-oh)* . . . . radio   _____
☐ **raketto** *(dah-ket-toh)* . . . . racket   _____
☐ **rasshiawā** *(dahsh-shee-ah-wāh)* . . . . rush hour   _____
☐ **raudosupiikā** *(dow-doh-soo-pēē-kāh)* . . . . loudspeaker   _____
☐ **referii** *(deh-feh-dēē)* . . . . referee   _____

71

Iku *(ee-koo)* go is another **hijō ni taisetsu na dōshi** important (P) for the **ryokōsha.** traveler If **anata wa** choose **jidōsha de** *(dyoh-kōh-shah)* **iku, koko ni** a few key **tango ga arimasu.** *(ee-koo)* go

kōsoku dōrō *(kōh-soh-koo) (dōh-dōh)* _____
freeway

renta kā *(ren-tah) (kāh)* _____
rental car

michi *(mee-chee)* _michi, michi_
road, street

renta kā ya *(ren-tah) (kāh)* _____
agency

dōri *(dōh-dee)* _____
avenue

kōtsū kippu *(kōh-tsōo) (keep-poo)* _____
traffic ticket

Koko ni four **hijō ni taisetsu** *(tie-seh-tsoo)* important opposites **arimasu.**

Ōsaka kara Kyōto made			
Shuppatsu jikoku	Densha	Tōchaku jikoku	Yukisaki
7:40	tokkyū	8:10	Kyōto
10:00	kyūkō	10:45	Kyōto
12:15	futsū	1:15	Kyōto
14:30	kyūkō	15:15	Kyōto
17:10	tokkyū	17:40	Kyōto

tōchaku *(tōh-chah-koo)* _tōchaku_
arrival

shuppatsu *(shoop-pah-tsoo)* _____
departure

gaikoku no *(guy-koh-koo)* _____
foreign (P)

kokunai *(koh-koo-nye)* _____
domestic

Let's learn the basic **ryokō no dōshi.** (P) Follow the same pattern **anata wa** have in previous Steps

tobimasu *(toh-bee-mahss)* = fly

chakuriku shimasu *(chah-koo-dee-koo) (shee-mahss)* = land

yoyaku shimasu *(yoy-yah-koo) (shee-mahss)* = reserve/book

_____

_____

_____

tsukimasu *(tsoo-kee-mahss)* = arrive

demasu *(deh-mahss)* = leave, depart

unten shimasu *(oon-ten) (shee-mahss)* = drive

_____ _demasu_ _____

norimasu *(noh-dee-mahss)* = board

orimasu *(oh-dee-mahss)* = disembark/ get out

norikaemasu *(noh-dee-kah-eh-mahss)* = transfer (vehicles)

_____

_____

_____

- ☐ **rekōdo** *(deh-kōh-doh)* . . . . record _____
- ☐ **remon** *(deh-mohn)* . . . . lemon _____
- ☐ **ribon** *(dee-bohn)* . . . . ribbon _____
- ☐ **robii** *(doh-bēē)* . . . . lobby _____
- ☐ **rubii** *(doo-bēē)* . . . . ruby _____

With **kono dōshi, anata wa** are ready for any **ryokō** *(dyoh-kōh)* anywhere. **Anata wa** should have no

mondai *(mohn-die)* with **kono dōshi,** just remember the basic "plug-in" formula **anata wa** have

problems

already learned. Use that knowledge to translate the **tsugi no** thoughts into **Nihongo.**

Kotae wa shita ni arimasu. *(shtah)*

below

1. I fly by airplane to Japan. _____

2. I transfer trains in Tokyo. _____

3. He lands in Osaka. _____

4. We arrive tomorrow. *Watashitachi wa ashita tsukimasu.*

5. You get out in Kyoto. _____

6. They drive to Nagasaki. _____

7. I leave tomorrow for Kobe. _____

8. She boards the train. _____

9. I book a trip. _____

Koko ni arimasu some **atarashii tango** *(ah-tah-dah-shēē)* for your **ryokō.** *(dyoh-kōh)* As always, write out the **tango**

new *travels*

and practice the sample sentences out loud.

hōmu *(hōh-moo)*

platform

eki *(eh-kee)*

train station

kūkō *(kōō-kōh)*

airport

kūkō, kūkō

Shitsurei shimasu. *(shee-tsoo-day) (shee-mahss)*

excuse me

Hōmu wa doko desu ka? *(hōh-moo)*

platform   where is

Shitsurei shimasu.

Eki wa doko desu ka? *(eh-kee)*

train station

Shitsurei shimasu.

Kūkō wa doko desu ka? *(kōō-kōh)*

airport

KOTAE	
9. **Watashi wa ryokō o yoyaku shimasu.**	
8. **Kanojo wa densha ni norimasu.**	4. **Watashitachi wa ashita tsukimasu.**
7. **Watashi wa ashita Kōbe ni demasu.**	3. **Kare wa Osaka ni chákuriku shimasu.**
6. **Karera wa Nagasaki ni unten shimasu.**	2. **Watashi wa Tōkyō ni densha o norikaemasu.**
5. **Anata wa Kyōto ni orimasu.**	1. **Watashi wa Nihon ni hikōki de tobimasu.**

(dyōh-guy)
ryōgae
money exchange

(foon-shee-tsoo)
funshitsu
lost (articles)

(jee-koh-koo-hyōh)
jikokuhyō
timetable

Ōsaka kara Kyōto made			
Shuppatsu jikoku	Densha	Tōchaku	Yukisaki jikoku
7:40	tokkyū	8:10	Kyōto
10:00	kyūkō	10:45	Kyōto
12:15	futsū	1:15	Kyōto
14:30	kyūkō	15:15	Kyōto
17:10	tokkyū	17:40	Kyōto

(shee-tsoo-day) (shee-mahss)
Shitsurei shimasu.
excuse me
(dyōh-guy)
Ryōgae wa doko desu ka?

Shitsurei shimasu.

(foon-shee-tsoo)
Funshitsu wa doko

desu ka?

Shitsurei shimasu.

(jee-koh-koo-hyōh)
Jikokuhyō wa doko

desu ka?

(tsoo-kaht-teh)(ee-mahss)
tsukatte imasu _____
being used/occupied

(eye-teh) (ee-mahss)
aite imasu _____
free/open

(seh-kee)
seki ___ *seki, seki, seki*
seat

(seh-kee)   (tsoo-kaht-teh)
Kono seki wa tsukatte imasu ka? _____
      seat   being used

_____

(eye-teh)
Kono seki wa aite imasu ka? _____
free

Practice writing out the *(tsoo-gee)* *(shee-tsoo-mohn)* **tsugi no shitsumon.** It will help **anata ato de.** *(ah-toh)(deh)*
following (P) questions   later

(shee-tsoo-day) (shee-mahss)
Shitsurei shimasu. *(toy-deh)* **Toire wa doko desu ka?** _____
excuse me   toilet
(kee-tsoo-en-shah)
Shitsurei shimasu. **Kitsuensha wa doko desu ka?** _____
                       smoking compartment
(mah-chee-eye-shee-tsoo)
Machiaishitsu wa doko desu ka? _____
waiting room
(oo-keh-tsoo-keh)
Hachi ban no uketsuke wa doko desu ka? _____
eight   number (P)   counter
(keen-en)
Kin'en desu ka? ___ *Kin'en desu ka?*
smoking prohibited

- sābisu *(sāh-bee-soo)* .... service
- saidā *(sigh-dāh)* .... cider
- sain *(sign)* .... sign
- sairen *(sigh-den)* .... siren
- sakkarin *(sahk-kah-deen)* .... saccharine

74

Increase your **ryokō no tango** *(dyoh-kōh)* (travel) (P) by writing out the **tango** below and practicing the sample

sentences out loud.

(yoo-kee)
yuki _____
to

Tōkyō yuki no densha wa doko desu ka?

(ahn-nye-joh)
annaijo _____
information desk

Annaijo wa doko desu ka?

(sen)
sen *sen, sen, sen*
track

Nana ban no sen wa doko desu ka?

(pōh-tāh)
pōtā _____
porter

Pōtā wa doko desu ka?

(gēh-toh)
gēto _____
gate

Nana ban no gēto wa doko desu ka?

densha no kippu *(keep-poo)* _____
train (P) ticket

Densha no kippu o kudasai.

Practice **kono tango** every day. **Anata wa** will be surprised how often **anata** will use

them. **Anata wa tsugi no** *(tsoo-gee)* following (P) paragraph o **yomimasu.** *(yoh-mee-mahss)* can read

---

Anata wa Nihon yuki no *(yoo-kee)* to (P) **hikōki ni** *(hee-kōh-kee)* airplane **norimasu.** *(noh-dee-mahss)* board **Anata wa en o motte imasu.** yen *(moht-teh)* have **Anata wa**
kippu to pasupōto *(toh)* and *(pah-soo-pōh-toh)* passport **mo motte imasu.** *(moh)* also **Anata no sūtsukēsu** *(sōō-tsoo-kēh-soo)* your suitcases are all packed. **Anata wa**
mō ryokōsha desu. *(mōh)* already *(dyoh-kōh-shah)* tourist **Anata wa ashita** *(ah-shtah)* tomorrow **kuji ni Nihon ni tsukimasu.** nine o'clock *(tsoo-kee-mahss)* arrive **Dōzo yoi ryokō o!** *(yoy)* have a good trip
Tanoshinde kudasai! *(tah-noh-sheen-deh)*
have fun

Ima anata have arrived and **anata** head for the **eki** *(eh-kee)* train station in order to get to **anata no saigo no** (P) *(sigh-goh)* final (P)
yukisaki. *(yoo-kee-sah-kee)* destination **Densha wa** come in many shapes, sizes **to** and speeds in **Nihon. Densha** that go

the fastest and travel the farthest are called **shinkansen.** *(sheen-kahn-sen)* bullet trains There are two kinds of

shinkansen: *(sheen-kahn-sen)* **hikari** *(hee-kah-dee)* express and **kodama.** *(koh-dah-mah)* ordinary There are also **junkyū,** *(joon-kyōō)* ordinary **kyūkō** *(kyōō-kōh)* express and **tokkyū** *(tohk-kyōō)* special express **densha.**
Some **densha** have **shokudōsha** *(shoh-koo-dōh-shah)* dining cars and some have **shindaisha.** *(sheen-die-shah)* sleeping cars All this will be indicated on

the **jikokuhyō,** *(jee-koh-koo-hyōh)* timetable but remember, **anata wa** know how to ask **shitsumon** *(shee-tsoo-mohn)* questions about **kono mono.**

Practice your possible **shitsumon** by writing out the **tsugi no** (P) samples.

Eki wa doko desu ka? *(eh-kee)* train station *Eki wa doko desu ka?*

Kono densha ni shokudōsha ga arimasu ka? *(shoh-koo-dōh-shah)* this train on dining car is there _____

Kono densha ni shindaisha ga arimasu ka? *(sheen-die-shah)* sleeping car _____

☐ **sandoicchi** *(sahn-doh-eet-chee)* .... sandwich _____
☐ **sarada** *(sah-dah-dah)* .... salad _____
☐ **semento** *(seh-men-toh)* .... cement _____
☐ **shampen** *(shahm-pen)* .... champagne _____
☐ **shinhonii** *(sheen-hoh-nēē)* .... symphony _____

What about inquiring about **kippu no nedan?** *(keep-poo)* *(neh-dahn)* **Anata wa** can ask **kono shitsumon,** too!

ticket (P) prices

ittō *(eet-tōh)* _itt̄ō_____ **nitō** *(nee-tōh)* _____

first-class   second-class

Ōsaka yuki *(yoo-kee)* **no kippu** *(keep-poo)* **wa ikura** *(ee-koo-dah)* **desu ka?** _____

to (P) ticket how much

Ittō desu ka? *(eet-tōh)* _____ **Nitō desu ka?** *(nee-tōh)* _____

first-class   second-class

katamichi *(kah-tah-mee-chee)* _____ **ōfuku** *(ōh-foo-koo)* _____

one-way   round-trip

Tōkyō yuki no kippu wa ikura desu ka? _____

Katamichi desu ka? *(kah-tah-mee-chee)* _____ **Ōfuku desu ka?** *(ōh-foo-koo)* _____

one-way   round-trip

What about times of **shuppatsu** *(shoop-pah-tsoo)* and **tōchaku.** *(tōh-chah-koo)* **Anata wa** can also ask **kono shitsumon.**

departures   arrivals

Nagoya yuki *(yoo-kee)* **no densha wa itsu** *(ee-tsoo)* **demasu** *(deh-mahss)* **ka?** _____

to (P) when leaves

Nagasaki yuki no hikōki *(hee-kōh-kee)* **wa itsu demasu** *(deh-mahss)* **ka?** _____

(P) airplane

Kōbe kara *(kah-dah)* **no hikōki wa itsu tsukimasu** *(tsoo-kee-mahss)* **ka?** _____

from (P) arrives

Nyūyōku *(nyōo-yōh-koo)* **kara no hikōki wa itsu tsukimasu** *(tsoo-kee-mahss)* **ka?** _____

(P)

Sapporo kara no densha wa itsu tsukimasu ka? _____

(P)

Anata wa have arrived in **Nihon.** **Ima anata wa eki** *(eh-kee)* **ni imasu.** **Ima wa doko** do **anata**

train station at are

want to go? In **Nihongo,** "would like to go" is **"ikitai desu."** *(ee-kee-tie)* **Ima** let's practice using

this **hijō** *(tie-seh-tsoo)* **ni taisetsu na tango.**

important (P)

Watashi wa Kyōto ni ikitai desu. *(ee-kee-tie)* _____

to would like to go

Watashi wa Ōsaka ni ikitai desu. *(ee-kee-tie)* _Watashi wa Ōsaka ni ikitai desu._

would like to go

Watashitachi wa Tōkyō ni ikitai desu. *(ee-kee-tie)* _____

(P)

Tōkyō yuki *(yoo-kee)* **no densha wa itsu** *(ee-tsoo)* **demasu** *(deh-mahss)* **ka?** _____

to (P) when leaves

Tōkyō yuki no kippu wa ikura *(ee-koo-dah)* **desu ka?** _____

(P) how much

Tōkyō yuki no kippu o kudasai. _____

(P)

With this practice, **anata wa** are off and running. **Kono ryokō** *(dyoh-kōh)* **no tango** will make your

travel (P)

holiday twice as enjoyable and at least three times as easy. Review the **atarashii tango** *(ah-tah-dah-shēē)* by

new

76 doing the **kurossuwādo** *(koo-dohs-soo-wāh-doh)* on page 77. Practice drilling yourself on this Step by selecting

crossword puzzle

other locations and asking your own **shitsumon** about **densha, basu** or **hikōki** that go

there. Select **atarashii tango** *(ah-tah-dah-shēē)* from **anata no jibiki** *(jee-bee-kee)* and practice asking **shitsumon** that

begin with

(doh-koh)	*(ee-tsoo)*	*(ee-koo-dah)*	*(nahn-jee)*
DOKO	**ITSU**	**IKURA**	**NANJI**
where	when	how much	what time

(P) dictionary

or making statements like

Watashi wa Tōkyō ni ikitai desu. *(ee-kee-tie)*
would like to go

Kōbe yuki no kippu o kudasai.

KUROSSUWĀDO

ACROSS

2. porter
6. train station
7. what time
8. departure
9. price
10. bus
12. seat
13. disembark, get out
15. airport
16. airplane
17. exit
19. round-trip
21. money exchange
23. gate
24. platform
26. bicycle
29. first-class
30. traveler
31. side entrance

DOWN

1. train
3. arrival
4. sleeping car
5. bullet train
11. dining car
14. travel
18. main entrance
20. one-way
21. entrance
22. free, open
25. boat
26. car
27. second-class
28. ticket

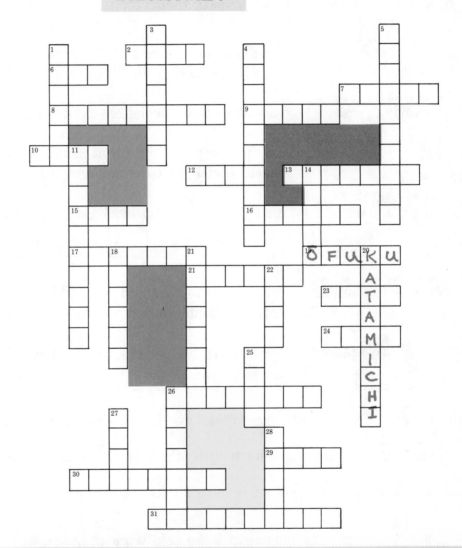

77

Step 18

Ima anata wa Nihon de anata no *(heh-yah)* **heya** ni imasu. **Onaka** *(oh-nah-kah)* **ga** **suite** *(soo-ee-teh)* **imasu.** Anata wa
your (P) room are in   stomach   empty

would like something to eat, but *(ēe)* **ii** **resutoran wa doko desu ka?** First of all, there are
good

different types of places to eat. Let's learn them.

(dess-toh-dahn) **resutoran**	= exactly what it says with a variety of meals and prices, usually specializing in Western dishes
(dyōh-dee-yah) *(dyōh-tay)* **ryōriya** /**ryōtei**	= **resutoran** that specializes exclusively in **Nihongo** dishes
(kees-sah-ten) **kissaten**	= a coffee shop/teahouse that usually serves light meals **to** snacks throughout the day and into the evening ^and
(oo-dohn-yah) *(soh-bah-yah)* **udonya** /**sobaya**	= a noodle shop that provides a variety of noodle dishes
(soo-shee)(yah) **sushi ya**	= **resutoran** that serves only **sashimi** *(sah-shee-mee)* and **sushi** *(soo-shee)* raw fish vinegared rice and fish
(bāh) *(kyah-bah-dēh)* *(soo-nahk-koo)* **bā** / **kyabarē** / **sunakku**	= comparable to bars and cocktail lounges in **Amerika,** serving only drinks and hors d'oeuvres
(bee-yah-gāh-den) **biyagāden**	= serves **biiru** and snacks, usually located on the rooftops of downtown buildings

Try all of them. Experiment. **Anata wa** have found *(ēe)* **ii resutoran.** **Anata wa resutoran ni**
good

(seh-kee) *(sah-gah-shee-mahss)*
seki o sagashimasu. Sharing **tēburu** with others is a common and **hijō ni** pleasant
seat   look for

(shōo-kahn)
shūkan in **Nihon.** If **anata wa** see a vacant **seki,** *(seh-kee)* just be sure to ask
custom   seat

(soo-mee-mah-sen) *(eye-teh)*
Sumimasen ga kono seki wa aite imasu ka?
sorry to bother you   but   free

If **anata wa** need a **menyū,** *(men-yōo)* catch the attention of **uētā** *(oo-ēh-tāh)* or **uētoresu** *(oo-ēh-toh-deh-soo)* and say
waiter   waitress

(choht-toh)
Chotto! Menyū o misete kudasai. *(mee-seh-teh)*
show

☐ **sōda** *(sōh-dah)*	soda
☐ **sōsu** *(sōh-soo)*	sauce
☐ **suchuwādesu** *(soo-choo-wāh-deh-soo)*	stewardess
☐ **sētā** *(sēh-tāh)*	sweater
☐ **sukejūru** *(soo-keh-jōo-doo)*	schedule

Nihonjin have three **shokuji** *(shoh-koo-jee)* a day, as well as snacks in **gogo.** *(goh-goh)*
Japanese (people)   meals   afternoon

chōshoku/asagohan *(chōh-shoh-koo) (ah-sah-goh-hahn)*	=	breakfast . . . In **hoteru no resutoran, kono shokuji** *(shoh-koo-jee)* usually consists of **kōhii** or **kōcha,** *(kōh-chah)* toast **to bata.** *(toh)* In **ryokan,** *(dyoh-kahn)* a traditional **Nihon no chōshoku,** *(chōh-shoh-koo)* consisting of **gohan,** *(goh-hahn)* seaweed, **shirumono,** *(shee-doo-moh-noh)* raw **tamago to sakana** *(tah-mah-goh) (sah-kah-nah)* is served.
hirugohan *(hee-doo-goh-hahn)*	=	lunch . . . . . Generally served from 11:30 to 14:00.
yūhan *(yōo-hahn)*	=	dinner . . . . . Generally served from 17:00 to 21:00 and sometimes later. After 21:00, snacks are usually served.

If **anata wa** look around in a **Nihon no resutoran, anata** will see that some **Nihon no shūkan** *(shōo-kahn)* are different from ours. **Hashi** *(hah-shee)* are generally used as eating utensils and **anata wa** will be seated on straw mats called **tatami.** *(tah-tah-mee)* Don't be surprised when **anata wa** are asked to remove your shoes. Only bare feet are allowed on **tatami.**

In **Nihon no resutoran, anata wa** will be greeted with **"Irasshaimase"** *(ee-dahsh-shy-mah-seh)* and, if **anata** hear the **uēta** *(ōo-eh-tāh)* say **"Dōzo,"** *(dōh-zoh)* it simply means that **anata** may start your **shokuji.** *(shoh-koo-jee)* Oftentimes, customers will say **"Itadakimasu"** *(ee-tah-dah-kee-mahss)* when they are served, meaning "I will receive the food."

Don't worry if **anata wa** cannot always read the **menyū.** In most **Nihon no resutoran,** plastic replicas of the food served in the **resutoran** are on display in a **mado.** *(mah-doh)* **Nedan** *(neh-dahn)* are also indicated in the **mado.** **Anata wa** can simply point out to the **uēta** *(oo-ēh-tāh)* or **uētoresu** *(oo-ēh-toh-deh-soo)* what **anata** would like to eat. **Oshokuji o dōzo!** *(oh-shoh-koo-jee)*
window   prices   meal   please (enjoy)

- ☐ **sukii** *(soo-kēē)* . . . . ski _____
- ☐ **sukuriin** *(soo-koo-dēēn)* . . . . screen _____
- ☐ **supōtsu** *(soo-pōh-tsoo)* . . . . sports _____
- ☐ **sūpu** *(sōo-poo)* . . . . soup (Western-style) _____
- ☐ **sutēki** *(soo-tēh-kee)* . . . . steak _____

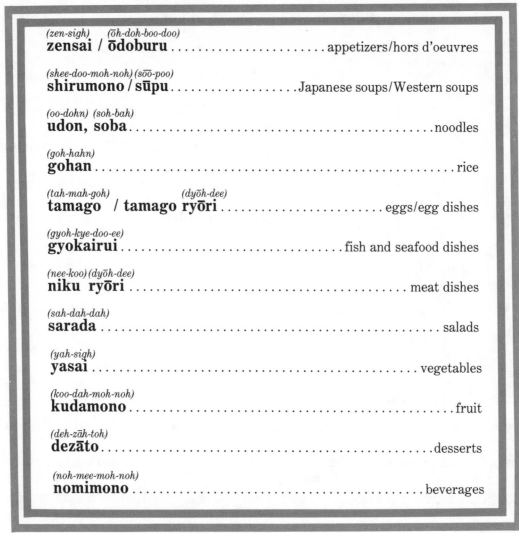

(zen-sigh) *(ōh-doh-boo-doo)*	
zensai / ōdoburu	appetizers/hors d'oeuvres
(shee-doo-moh-noh) (sōō-poo)	
shirumono / sūpu	Japanese soups/Western soups
(oo-dohn) (soh-bah)	
udon, soba	noodles
(goh-hahn)	
gohan	rice
(tah-mah-goh) *(dyōh-dee)*	
tamago / tamago ryōri	eggs/egg dishes
(gyoh-kye-doo-ee)	
gyokairui	fish and seafood dishes
(nee-koo) (dyōh-dee)	
niku ryōri	meat dishes
(sah-dah-dah)	
sarada	salads
(yah-sigh)	
yasai	vegetables
(koo-dah-moh-noh)	
kudamono	fruit
(deh-zāh-toh)	
dezāto	desserts
(noh-mee-moh-noh)	
nomimono	beverages

Most **resutoran** also offer **tokushoku na ryōri** *(toh-koo-shoh-koo)* (special) *(dyōh-dee)* (dishes) prepared by the chef or **shokuji** *(shoh-koo-jee)* (meals) prepared

with regional ingredients. One **Nihon no** (P) speciality **anata wa** may want to try is

tempura *(tehm-poo-dah)* — **sakana** *(sah-kah-nah)* (fish) **to yasai** *(yah-sigh)* (and vegetables) dipped in batter and deep-fried. If **anata wa** want to be very

Nihon (Japanese) **teki,** *(teh-kee)* (like) add a little soy sauce flavored with **sake** to your **tempura.**

Ima for a preview of delights to come ... At the back of **kono hon, anata** will find a

sample **Nihon no menyū.** (P) Read the **menyū** and learn the **atarashii tango.** *(ah-tah-dah-shēē)* When **anata**

wa are ready to leave for **Nihon,** cut out the **menyū,** fold it and carry it in your pocket,

wallet or purse. **Anata wa** can go into any **resutoran** and feel prepared. (May **watashi**

suggest studying the **menyū** after, and not before, **anata** have eaten!)

☐ **tabako** *(tah-bah-koh)*	tobacco	_____
☐ **taipu** *(tie-poo)*	type	_____
— **taipuraitā** *(tie-poo-die-tāh)*	typewriter	_____
☐ **taiya** *(tie-yah)*	tire	_____
80 ☐ **takushii** *(tah-koo-shēē)*	taxi	_____

In addition, learning **tsugi no tango** *(tsoo-gee)* should help **anata** to identify what kind of meat

(ah-doo-ee)
arui wa poultry **anata wa** **chūmon shimasu** and **dō** it will be prepared.
or   *(chōo-mohn)* *(shee-mahss)* *(dōh)*
                order   how

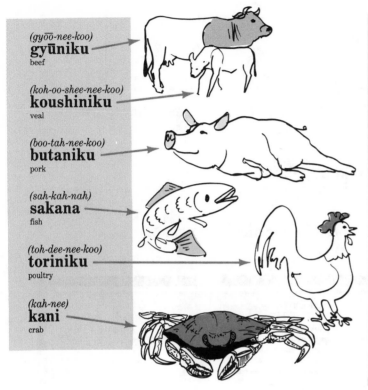

(gyōo-nee-koo)
gyūniku
beef

(koh-oo-shee-nee-koo)
koushiniku
veal

(boo-tah-nee-koo)
butaniku
pork

(sah-kah-nah)
sakana
fish

(toh-dee-nee-koo)
toriniku
poultry

(kah-nee)
kani
crab

(nah-mah-moh-noh) **namamono**	=	raw
(nee-tah) **nita**	=	cooked
(tsoo-keh-moh-noh) **tsukemono ni shita**	=	pickled
(yoo-deh-tah) **yudeta**	=	boiled
(moo-shtah) **mushita**	=	steamed
(yi-tah) **yaita**	=	baked/grilled
(ee-tah-meh-tah) *(ah-geh-tah)* **itameta** /**ageta**	=	fried

Anata wa will also get **shirumono, gohan to tsukemono** with **anata no shokuji.** A day
   (shee-doo-moh-noh) *(goh-hahn)* *(toh)* *(tsoo-keh-moh-noh)*   *(shoh-koo-jee)*
         soup   rice   and   pickled vegetables   (P)   meal

(ee-chee-bah)   *(yah-siqh)* *(koo-dah-moh-noh)*
at **ichiba** will teach you **namae** of different kinds of **yasai to kudamono,** plus it will be a
market   vegetables   fruit

delightful experience for **anata.** **Anata wa** can always consult **anata no menyū** guide at

the back of **kono hon** if **anata wa** forget **tadashii namae.** **Ima anata wa** have decided
                                   (tah-dah-shēē)
                                   correct

what **anata** would like to eat and **uētā ga kimasu.**
                           (kee-mahss)
                           comes

- [ ] **tanku** *(tahn-koo)* . . . . tank
- [ ] **taoru** *(tah-oh-doo)* . . . . towel
- [ ] **tāru** *(tāh-doo)* . . . . tar
- [ ] **tēburu** *(tēh-boo-doo)* . . . . table
- [ ] **tenisu** *(teh-nee-soo)* . . . . tennis

Don't forget to treat yourself to **Nihon no dezāto.** *(deh-zāh-toh)* **Anata wa** would not want to miss out

on trying the *(tsoo-gee)* **tsugi no dezāto.**

following (P)

(P) dessert

(mee-tsoo-mah-meh) **mitsumame** boiled peas, fruit and gelatin in a sweet syrup	*(ahn-mee-tsoo)* **anmitsu** boiled peas with honey and bean jam
(yōh-kahn) **yōkan** cake made with sweetened red beans	*(zen-zye)* **zenzai** pounded rice topped with sweetened red beans

---

After completing **anata no shokuji,** call the **uētā** and pay just as **anata** have already

learned in Step 16:

Kanjōgaki o kudasai.

(shtah) **Shita ni wa** a sample **menyū** to help **anata** prepare for **anata no ryokō.** *(dyoh-kōh)*

below   trip

TEIKOKU RESUTORAN

MENYŪ

ZENSAI/ŌDOBURU (hors d'oeuvres)

ika no shiokara (salted cuttlefish guts)	¥1000
katsuo no shiokara (salted bonito guts)	1000
kanisu (vinegared crab)	1500
kaiso moriawase (selected seaweed)	1000

SHIRUMONO (soup)

akadashi (red bean paste soup)	150
misoshiru (white bean paste soup)	150
suimono (clear soup)	100
oden (stew of vegetables, fish-paste cakes and fried foods)	200

GYOKAIRUI (fish and seafood dishes)

SASHIMI (sliced raw fish)

maguro (tuna)	2000
ebi (shrimp)	3000
tako (octopus)	4000
ikura (salmon roe)	4500
ika (squid)	5000

SUSHI (vinegared fish and rice)

inarizushi (fried beancurd stuffed with vinegared rice)	1500
makizushi (fish and rice rolled in seaweed)	1000
nigirizushi (hand-pressed rice ball with seafood)	1000
chirashizushi (pilaf-style rice with egg topping)	3000

TEMPURA (deep-fried fish and vegetables) 2500

SAKANA YAKI (broiled/grilled fish) 2500

NIKU RYŌRI (meat dishes)

sukiyaki (beef and vegetables in sauce)	1200
shabu shabu (beef and vegetables in seasoned broth)	1500
teppan yaki (grilled meat and vegetables)	1500
yakitori (barbecued chicken)	500
tonkatsu (deep-fried pork cutlet)	1200

UDON/SOBA (noodles)

tempura udon (noodles in broth with deep-fried prawns and vegetables)	500
kitsune udon (noodles in broth with fried beancurd)	500
nabeyaki udon (seafood and fish cakes in broth)	800
yakisoba (sauced noodles and vegetables)	500

TAMAGO RYŌRI (egg dishes)

tamagoyaki (omelette)	800
okonomiyaki (meat and vegetable omelette)	800
tamagodofu (custard)	800

GOHAN (rice)

tendon (shrimp and vegetable **tempura** over rice)	1000
unadon (eel over rice)	1500
katsudon (pork cutlet over rice)	800
oyakodon (chicken and egg over rice)	800
tamagodon (egg over rice)	800

NOMIMONO (beverages)

kōcha (black tea)	500
ocha (green tea)	200
kōhii (coffee)	500
miruku (milk)	500
jūsu (juice)	400
Koka Kōra (Coca-Cola)	400
biiru (beer)	700
budōshu (wine)	1500
sake (rice wine)	1000

☐ **tento** *(ten-toh)* .... tent _____

☐ **tēpu** *(tēh-poo)* .... tape _____

☐ **terebijon** *(teh-dee-bee-jone)* .... television _____

☐ **tomato** *(toh-mah-toh)* .... tomato _____

☐ **ton** *(tohn)* .... ton _____

82

In **Nihon, chōshoku** *(chōh-shoh-koo)* is a **hijō ni** simple **shokuji**. **Anata wa** can eat in **hoteru no shokudo** *(shoh-koo-doh)*
breakfast   very (P)   (P) dining room

arui wa resutoran. A Western-style **chōshoku** is usually provided for **ryokōsha.** *(dyoh-kōh-shah)*
or   tourists

Remember that a traditional **Nihon no chōshoku,** consisting of **gohan**, seaweed **to sakana**, *(sah-kah-nah)*
(P)   rice   and fish

is served in **ryokan.**

Chōshoku 1 . . . . ¥500

kōhii arui wa kōcha *(kōh-chah)*
black tea

(dōh-doo)(pahn)
rōru pan to bata
rolls

Chōshoku 3 . . . . ¥1000

jūsu arui wa miruku,   kōhii arui wa kōcha

(tōh-soo-toh)   *(hah-moo)(eg-goo-zoo)*
tōsuto to bata,   **hamu egguzu**
toast   ham and eggs

Chōshoku 2 . . . . ¥800

orenji jūsu, kōhii arui wa kōcha

pan to bata

(meh-dah-mah) (yah-kee) (tah-mah-goh)
medama yaki tamago arui wa
fried   eggs
(ee-dee)
iri   tamago
scrambled eggs

(noh-mee-moh-noh)
Nomimono
beverages

kōhii ¥250

kōcha ¥250

orenji jūsu ¥150

miruku ¥150

☐ **tonneru** *(tohn-neh-doo)* . . . . tunnel
☐ **torakku** *(toh-dahk-koo)* . . . . truck
☐ **tōsuta** *(tōh-soo-tah)* . . . . toaster
☐ **toranku** *(toh-dahn-koo)* . . . . trunk
☐ **torofii** *(toh-doh-fēē)* . . . . trophy

Step 19

(den-wah)
Denwa
telephone

Nihon ni, nani is different about **denwa?** Well, **anata wa** never notice such **mono** until

anata want to use them. With **denwa, anata wa yoyaku** *(yoy-yah-koo)* **shimasu.** *(shee-mahss)* **Anata wa gekijō** *(geh-kee-jōh)* no
reservations   make   theater   (P)

kippu mo *(moh)* **kaimasu.** *(kye-mahss)* With **denwa, anata wa** can contact **anata no otomodachi,** *(oh-toh-moh-dah-chee)* check on
          also   buy   (P)   friends

depāto *(deh-pāh-toh)* **no jikan,** *(jee-kahn)* call for **takushii,** make emergency **tsūwa** *(tsōō-wah)* and a lot of **mono** that
department store (P) hours   calls

watashitachi wa shimasu *(shee-mahss)* every day. When **anata wa** use **kōshū** *(kōō-shōō)* **denwa,** make sure you
                    do   public

have plenty of **otsuri** *(oh-tsoo-dee)* and don't forget to speak **yukkuri** *(yook-koo-dee)* and clearly.
                change   slowly

Nihon ni, having a **denwa** in **anata no hoteru no heya** *(heh-yah)* is not as common as **Amerika ni.**
                                                    (P)   room

Anata wa denwa o sagashimasu *(sah-gah-shee-mahss)* on the **michi,** *(mee-chee)* in **hoteru no robii,** *(doh-bēē)* **arui wa** at the
                    look for   street   (P)   lobby

yūbinkyoku. *(yōō-bean-kyoh-koo)* **Nihon ni,** there are **denwa** *(den-wah)* **kyoku** *(kyoh-koo)* in which **anata** will also find **kōshū denwa.** *(kōh-shōō)*
post office   telephone   offices   public

Koko ni Nihon no kōshū denwa ga arimasu.

Amerika to Nihon ni, denwa bokusu wa *(bohk-soo)*
                                                        booths
nitemasu ga, *(nee-teh-mahss)* as **anata** will see, there are
are similar   but

some differences. This is one of those

moments when **anata** realize,

Watashi wa Amerika ni imasen. *(ee-mah-sen)*
                          am not

So let's learn how to operate **Nihon no**
                                        (P)

denwa.

84

The different types of **denwa** in **Nihon** are easily identifiable by **iro**. *(ee-doh)* *(ah-kye)* **Akai denwa arui wa**
color   red

(moh-moh-ee-doh)
momoiro denwa are found in **bā, resutoran** and other **kōshū** places. *(kōh-shōō)* **Aoi denwa** are found *(ah-oy)*
pink   public   blue

(bohk-soo)
in **denwa bokusu** and can be used to make either inter-city **tsūwa** within **Nihon** or *(tsōō-wah)*
                                                                        calls

(chōh-kyoh-dee)
chōkyori   denwa. Anata wa will also see **kiiroi denwa** *(kēē-doy)* which are generally used for
long-distance/overseas telephone (calls)   yellow

(tsōō-wah)   *(shtah)*
inter-city **tsūwa** in **Nihon**. **Shita** are the instructions for making **denwa**.
                            below   telephone (calls)

SHINAI DENWA
(shee-nye)
local   telephone (calls)

Jū en o iremasu. Bangō o mawashimasu.
ten   insert   dial

San pun ato, ni chūi no chimu o kikoemasu.
three minutes after   warning (P)   you hear

Motto jū en dama o iremasu. Denwa o tsuzukeraremasu.
more   coins   insert   you continue

Denwa ga owatta ato de, nokotta jū en dama ga modorimasu.
            you finish   after   remaining   return

(chōh-kyoh-dee)
Chōkyori denwa to foreign countries can be made from **aoi denwa** *(ah-oy)* only. The following
                                                           blue

should help to familiarize **anata** with making **chōkyori denwa,** *(chōh-kyoh-dee)* in case **anata wa** ever have

to call home to **Amerika**. It is very similar to the process used in **Amerika** for calling

overseas. Also keep in mind that **anata wa hoteru no heya kara mo denwa ga dekimasu.** *(deh-kee-mahss)*
                                              (P)   room   from   also   can make

---

CHŌKYORI DENWA
(chōh-kyoh-dee)
overseas   telephone (call)

Kokusai Denwa Denden (KDD) Kosha ni denwa o kakemasu.
International Telephone Telegraph   Service to   make call

Kōkanshu ga denwa no toritsugi o shimasu.
operator   (P) connection   makes

Eigo	Nihongo	Eigo	Nihongo
telephone	= **denwa**	overseas telephone (call)	= **chōkyori denwa** *(chōh-kyoh-dee)*
telephone booth	= **denwa bokusu** *(bohk-soo)*	local telephone (call)	= **shinai denwa** *(shee-nye)*
telephone directory/book	= **denwa chō** *(chōh)*	public telephone	= **kōshū denwa** *(kōh-shōō)*
telephone conversation	= **denwa no kaiwa** *(kye-wah)*	operator	= **kōkanshu** *(kōh-kahn-shoo)*

Ima anata wa can make **denwa no tsūwa** *(tsōō-wah)* in **Nihon**. But what do **anata wa iimasu** *(ee-mahss)*
(P) calls *say*

when **anata** finally get through to your party? The **hito** *(hee-toh)* who answers the **denwa** will
person

usually say, "Moshi, moshi," *(moh-shee)* when **kare** picks up the **reshiiba**. *(deh-shee-bah)* **Anata wa** should identify
hello *receiver*

yourself by giving **anata no namae** and then ask for the **hito** you wish to speak with.

"Moshi, moshi. Tanaka to mōshimasu ga. *(mōh-shee-mahss)* Sumimasen ga Suzukisan wa irasshaimasu ka?" *(soo-mee-mah-sen)* *(ee-dahsh-shy-mahss)*
(P) *speaking* *sorry to bother you* *but* *is in*

When saying goodbye, **anata wa iimasu**, *(ee-mahss)* "Sayonara" *(sigh-yoh-nah-dah)* **arui wa** "De wa mata." *(mah-tah)*
say *goodbye* *again*

Koko ni some sample **denwa no kaiwa ga arimasu**. *(kye-wah)* In **Nihongo**, "would like to make a

telephone call" translates as "denwa o kaketai desu." *(kah-keh-tie)* **Ima** practice using these **hijō ni**

taisetsu na tango *(tie-seh-tsoo)* by saying the following sentences out loud and then filling in the blanks
important *(P)*

shita. *(shtah)*
below

Tōkyō Daigaku ni denwa o kaketai desu. *(die-gah-koo)* *(kah-keh-tie)* _____
university *to* *telephone call* *I would like to make*

Shikago ni denwa o kaketai desu. *(shee-kah-goh)* _____
Chicago

Itosan ni denwa o kaketai desu. _____
Mr. Ito

Suzukisan ni denwa o kaketai desu. _____

Narita Kūkō ni denwa o kaketai desu. *(nah-dee-tah) (kōō-kōh)* _____
airport

Shinai denwa o kaketai desu. *(shee-nye)* _____
local

Chōkyori denwa o kaketai desu. *(chōh-kyoh-dee)* _____

Senpō barai no denwa o kaketai desu. *(sen-pōh) (bah-die)* _____
collect *call*

Kōshū denwa wa doko desu ka? *(kōh-shōō)* _____
public

Denwa chō wa doko desu ka? *(chōh)* _____
directory

Denwa bangō wa 473-6440 desu. _____

86 **Koko ni** another possible **kaiwa ga arimasu**. Listen to the **tango** and how they are used.

Thomas:	*(moh-shee)* **Moshi, moshi.** **Takahasi to mōshimasu.** **Sumimasen ga Yamamotosan**
	hello *(moh-shee-mahss)* (P) speaking *(soo-mee-mah-sen)* sorry to bother you but Mr. Yamamoto
	(ee-dahsh-shy-mahss) **wa irasshaimasu ka?**
	is in
Hisho:	*(hee-shoh)* *(choht-toh)* *(maht-teh)* **Chotto matte kudasai.** *(soo-mee-mah-sen)* **Sumimasen.** *(hah-nah-shee-chōō)* **Ima hanashichū desu.**
	secretary just wait sorry line busy
Thomas:	*(mōh)* *(ee-chee-doh)* **Mō ichido kudasai.** **Nihongo o** *(soo-koh-shee)* **sukoshi** *(hah-nah-shee-mahss)* **hanashimasu.** *(moht-toh)* **Motto**
	more once little speak more
	(yook-koo-dee) **yukkuri kudasai.**
	slowly
Hisho:	**Sumimasen.** *(hah-nah-shee-chōō)* **Ima hanashichū desu.**
	line busy line busy
Thomas:	*(dōh-moh)* *(sigh-yoh-nah-dah)* **Dōmo. Sayonara.**
	thanks goodbye

Koko ni another **denwa no kaiwa ga arimasu.**
                                    (P)

Christine:	**Watashi wa Kyōto no** *(jōh-hōh)* **jōhō** *(hoh-shēē)* **ga hoshii desu.** *(ee-shah)* **Isha no Tanakasan**
	(P) information would like doctor (P)
	no denwa bangō o kudasai.
Kōkanshu:	*(kōh-kahn-shoo)* **Bangō wa (075) 223-4476 desu.**
	operator
Christine:	**Bangō o** *(mōh)* **mō** *(ee-chee-doh)* **ichido kudasai.**
	more once
Kōkanshu:	**Bangō wa (075) 223-4476 desu.**
Christine:	**Dōmo** *(ah-dee-gah-tōh)* **arigatō** *(goh-zye-mahss)* **gozaimasu.** **Sayonara.**
	thank you very much
Kōkanshu:	*(dōh)* *(ee-tah-shee-mah-shtay)* **Dō itashimashite.** **Sayonara.**
	you're welcome

Ima anata wa are ready to use any **Nihon no denwa.** Just take it *(yook-koo-dee)* **yukkuri** and speak clearly.
                                      (P)   slowly

Don't forget that **anata wa** can always ask **shitsumon . . .**

(shee-nye) **Shinai denwa wa** *(ee-koo-dah)* **ikura desu ka?** _____
local   how much

Tōkyō e *(eh)* **no** *(chōh-kyoh-dee)* **chōkyori denwa wa ikura desu ka?** _____
        to (P) long-distance

Amerika e no chōkyori denwa wa ikura desu ka? _____
              (P)

Kōbe e no chōkyori denwa wa ikura desu ka? _____
       (P)

Also don't forget that **anata wa jū en** *(dah-mah)* **dama ga** *(ee-dee-mahss)* **irimasu** for *(kōh-shōō)* **kōshū denwa.**
                                      coins   need   public

87

Step 20

(chee-kah-teh-tsoo)
Chikatetsu
subway

In **Nihongo, chikatetsu** *(chee-kah-teh-tsoo)* means "underground railway" or "subway." Like **Amerika, shuyō** *(shoo-yōh)* major **toshi** *(toh-shee)* cities in **Nihon** have **chikatetsu** *(chee-kah-teh-tsoo)* subways. (**Anata wa** will find **chikatetsu** in **Tōkyō, Ōsaka, Nagoya, Yokohama** and **Sapporo.**) In **motto chiisa** *(chēe-sah)* smaller **na toshi** *(toh-shee)* cities **, basu, densha to takushii** and are **hijō ni benri** *(ben-dee)* very convenient forms of transportation. **Takushii** can be hailed from the **michi** *(mee-chee)* street or found at most **shuyō** *(shoo-yōh)* major **hoteru to densha no eki.** *(eh-kee)* and (P) stations There are also **takushii noriba** *(noh-dee-bah)* stands in front of many **Nihon no depāto.** *(deh-pāh-toh)* (P) department stores Let's learn how to take the **chikatetsu, basu arui wa takushii.** *(chee-kah-teh-tsoo)* subway or

Practice the **tsugi no tango** by saying them aloud and writing them in the blanks **shita.** (P)

(chee-kah-teh-tsoo)
chikatetsu

(tah-koo-shee)
takushii

(bah-soo)
basu

basu

(dyōh-keen)
ryōkin = (the) fare _____

(tay-dyōō-joh)
teiryūjo = (the) stop _____

(sen)
sen = (the) line *sen, sen, sen, sen, sen*

(oon-ten-shoo)
untenshu = (the) driver _____

(keep-poo) (kee-dee)
kippu kiri = (the) ticket collector _____

Let's also review the **ryokō no dōshi** *(dōh-shee)* (P) verbs at this point.

(noh-dee-mahss)
norimasu = board *norimasu, norimasu*

(oh-dee-mahss)
orimasu = disembark _____

(noh-dee-kah-eh-mahss)
norikaemasu = to transfer _____

(dyoh-kōh) (shee-mahss)
88 **ryokō shimasu** = travel _____

(chee-zoo)
Chizu displaying the various **sen to teiryūjo** are available at most **shuyō na eki** and even
maps   *(sen)*   *(tay-dyōō-joh)*   lines   stops   *(shoo-yōō)*   *(eh-kee)*   major   (P)   stations

at some **hoteru.** **Sen** are color-coded to help **anata** find your **yukisaki.** **Anata wa kippu o**
(yoo-kee-sah-kee)   destination

(kye-mahss)   *(ee-dee-goo-chee)*
kaimasu from a vending machine at the **eki no iriguchi.** **Kippu** will be punched when
buy   entrance

(chee-kah-teh-tsoo)   *(noh-dee-mahss)*
anata wa chikatetsu ni norimasu. Be sure to keep **anata no kippu,** because it will be
subway   board

(deh-goo-chee)   *(shee-soo-teh-moo)*   *(oh-tsoo-dee)*
collected at the **eki no deguchi.** For the **basu no shisutemu,** be sure to have **otsuri** with
(P)   exit   (P)   system   change

(oon-ten-shoo)   *(hah-die-mahss)*   *(noh-dee-mahss)*
anata. **Anata wa untenshu o haraimasu** when **anata wa basu ni norimasu.** **Ima** take a
driver   pay   board

look at the **shita no chizu.**
(P)   map

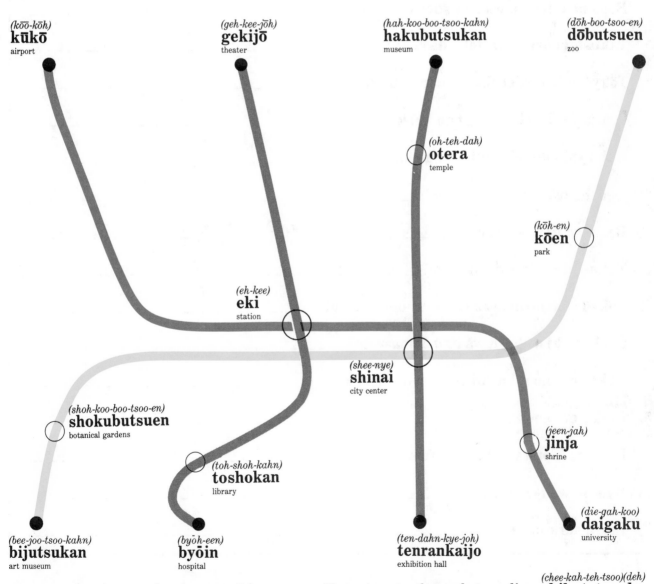

(kōō-kōh)
kūkō
airport

(geh-kee-jōh)
gekijō
theater

(hah-koo-boo-tsoo-kahn)
hakubutsukan
museum

(dōh-boo-tsoo-en)
dōbutsuen
zoo

(oh-teh-dah)
otera
temple

(kōh-en)
kōen
park

(eh-kee)
eki
station

(shee-nye)
shinai
city center

(shoh-koo-boo-tsoo-en)
shokubutsuen
botanical gardens

(toh-shoh-kahn)
toshokan
library

(jeen-jah)
jinja
shrine

(die-gah-koo)
daigaku
university

(bee-joo-tsoo-kahn)
bijutsukan
art museum

(byōh-een)
byōin
hospital

(ten-dahn-kye-joh)
tenrankaijo
exhibition hall

The same basic set of **tango to shitsumon** will see **anata** through traveling **chikatetsu de,**
(chee-kah-teh-tsoo)(deh)   subway   by

basu de, densha de, takushii de or even **jidōsha de.**

Naturally, the first **shitsumon wa "doko" desu.**
(shee-tsoo-mohn) *(doh-koh)*
question   where

(chee-kah-teh-tsoo) *(eh-kee)*
Chikatetsu no eki wa doko desu ka?
subway   (P)   station
(tay-dyōō-joh)
Basu no teiryūjo wa doko desu ka?
(P)   stop
(noh-dee-bah)
Takushii noriba wa doko desu ka?
stand

Practice the **tsugi no shitsumon** out loud **sore kara** write them in the blanks to the **migi.**
(tsoo-gee)   *(mee-gee)*
following (P)   and   then   right

(chee-kah-teh-tsoo) *(eh-kee)*
1. **Chikatetsu no eki wa doko desu ka?** _____
   subway   station
   (tay-dyōō-joh)
   Basu no teiryūjo wa doko desu ka? _____
   (P)   stop
   (noh-dee-bah)
   Takushii noriba wa doko desu ka?_____

   (yoo-kee)   *(nahn)* *(kye)* *(kee-mahss)*
2. **Tōkyō yuki no densha wa nan kai kimasu ka?** _____
   to   (P)   how often comes

   Ōsaka yuki no basu wa nan kai kimasu ka?_____
   (P)
   (kōō-kōh)
   Kūkō yuki no takushii wa nan kai kimasu ka? _____
   airport

   (ee-tsoo)(deh-mahss)
3. **Densha wa itsu demasu ka?** _____
   when leaves

   Basu wa itsu demasu ka? *Basu wa itsu demasu ka?*

   Takushii wa itsu demasu ka? _____

   (yoo-kee)   *(ee-tsoo)* *(deh-mahss)*
4. **Tōkyō yuki no densha wa itsu demasu ka?** _____
   to   (P)   when leaves

   Ōsaka yuki no basu wa itsu demasu ka? _____
   (P)

   Kūkō yuki no takushii wa itsu demasu ka? _____
   airport   (P)
   (chee-kah-teh-tsoo)   *(keep-poo)*   *(ee-koo-dah)*
5. **Chikatetsu no kippu wa ikura desu ka?** _____
   subway   (P) ticket   how much

   Basu no kippu wa ikura desu ka? _____

   (dyoh-keen)
   Ryokin wa ikura desu ka? _____
   fare
   (hah-die-mahss)
   Ikura haraimasu ka?_____
   I pay

Ima that **anata wa** are in the swing of things, practice the **tsugi no** patterns aloud,
(P)

substituting **"basu"** for **"chikatetsu"** and so on.
(chee-kah-teh-tsoo)

1. *(chee-kah-teh-tsoo)* *(keep-poo)* *(kye-mahss)*
   Chikatetsu no kippu wa doko de kaimasu ka? Basu no kippu wa doko de
   subway (P) ticket where at buy (P) ticket

   kaimasu ka? Densha no kippu wa doko de kaimasu ka?
   train (P) ticket

2. *(yoo-kee)* *(chee-kah-teh-tsoo)* *(ee-tsoo)* *(deh-mahss)* *(die-gah-koo)* *(chee-kah-teh-tsoo)*
   Tōkyō yuki no chikatetsu wa itsu demasu ka? Daigaku yuki no chikatetsu wa
   to (P) subway when leaves university to (P) subway

   (ee-tsoo) *(tay-koh-koo)* *(chee-kah-teh-tsoo)* *(nah-dee-tah)* *(kōō-kōh)*
   itsu demasu ka? Teikoku Hoteru yuki no chikatetsu wa? Narita Kūkō yuki no
   imperial (P) airport (P)

   (oh-teh-dah) *(kōh-en)*
   chikatetsu wa? Otera yuki no chikatetsu wa? Kōen yuki no chikatetsu wa?
   temple (P) park (P)

3. *(koo-kōh)* *(chee-kah-teh-tsoo)* *(eh-kee)*
   Kūkō yuki no chikatetsu no eki wa doko desu ka?
   airport to (P) subway (P) station where is

   (geh-kee-jōh)
   Gekijō yuki no chikatetsu no eki wa doko desu ka?
   theater (P) (P)

   (shee-nye) *(tay-dyōō-joh)*
   Shinai yuki no basu no teiryūjo wa doko desu ka?
   city center (P) (P) stop

   (dōh-boo-tsoo-en) *(tay-dyōō-joh)*
   Dōbutsuen yuki no basu no teiryūjo wa doko desu ka?
   zoo (P) (P)

   (bee-joo-tsoo-kahn) *(eh-kee)*
   Bijutsukan yuki no chikatetsu no eki wa doko desu ka?
   art museum (P) (P)

   (hah-koo-boo-tsoo-kahn)
   Hakubutsukan yuki no chikatetsu no eki wa doko desu ka?
   museum (P) (P)

   (eh-kee) *(tay-dyōō-joh)*
   Eki yuki no basu no teiryūjo wa doko desu ka?
   station (P) (P)

   (die-gah-koo) *(tay-dyōō-joh)*
   Daigaku yuki no basu no teiryūjo wa doko desu ka?
   university (P) (P)

   (shoh-koo-boo-tsoo-en)
   Shokubutsuen yuki no chikatetsu no eki wa doko desu ka?
   botanical gardens (P) (P)

(tsoo-gee) *(eep-pahn-teh-kee)* *(kye-wah)* *(mee-gee)*
Ima read the **tsugi no ippanteki na kaiwa** and write it in the blanks to the **migi.**
following (P) typical (P) right

(die-gah-koo) *(chee-kah-teh-tsoo)*
Tōkyō Daigaku yuki no chikatetsu wa nani sen desu ka? _____
university to (P) subway what line

(ah-kye)
Akai sen desu. _Akai sen desu._
red

(nahn) *(kye)* *(kee-mahss)*
Chikatetsu wa nan kai kimasu ka? _____
how often comes

(foon) *(oh-kee)*
Go fun oki desu. _____
five minutes every

(noh-dee-kye-mahss)
Norikaimasu ka? _____
I transfer

(hi) *(eh-kee)*
Hai. Tōkyō Eki de norikaimasu. _____
yes station at

(dyoh-kōh) *(doh-noh)* *(goo-die)* *(kah-kah-dee-mahss)*
Ryokō wa dono gurai kakarimasu ka? _____
trip how long takes

(nee-jōō-goh) *(foon)*
Nijūgo fun kakarimasu. _Nijūgo fun kakarimasu._
25 minutes

(ee-koo-dah)
Kippu wa ikura desu ka? _____
how much

(yohn-hyah-koo)
Yonhyaku en desu. _____
400

Can **anata wa** translate the **tsugi no** thoughts into **Nihongo**? **Kotae wa shita ni arimasu.** *(shtah)*
(P)   below

1. Where is the subway station? _____

2. How much is a ticket? _____

3. How often do the buses come? _____

4. Where do I buy a subway ticket? _____

5. Where is the bus stop? _____

6. Where is the taxi stand?_____

7. Do I transfer? *norikaimasu ka?* _____

8. Where do I transfer? _____

Koko ni atarashii dōshi ga arimasu.

(ah-die-mahss)   *(oo-shee-nye-mahss)*   *(kah-kah-dee-mahss)*
araimasu = wash   **ushinaimasu** = lose   **kakarimasu** = take (time)

araimasu _____   _____   _____

Anata wa know the basic "plug-in" formula, so translate the **tsugi no** thoughts with these
(P)

atarashii dōshi. Kono kotae mo shita ni arimasu.
also

1. I wash the jacket. _____

2. You lose the book. _____

3. It takes 25 minutes. _____

4. It takes three hours by car. _____

5. What subway line goes to the city center? _____

6. What subway line goes to the park? _____

(oo-dee-mahss)   (toh)   (kye-mahss)

Urimasu to Kaimasu
sell   and   buy

(guy-koh-koo)
Gaikoku ni, shopping is **hijō ni omoshiroi.** The simple, everyday task of buying a **rittoru**
foreign country   (P) interesting   liter

(deen-goh)
no miruku arui wa ringo becomes a challenge that **anata** should **ima** be able to meet
(P)   or   apple

quickly and easily. Of course, **anata wa** will purchase **omiyage, kitte to hagaki** but don't
(oh-mee-yah-geh) souvenirs   and

forget the many other **mono,** ranging from shoelaces to **asupirin,** that **anata** might need
(ah-soo-pee-deen) aspirin

unexpectedly. Do **anata wa** understand the difference between a **panya** and a **honya? Iie?**
(pahn-yah) bakery   *(hohn-yah)* bookstore   *(ee-eh)* no

Let's learn about **Nihon no mise. Shita wa Tōkyō no chizu desu.**
(mee-seh) (P) stores   *(chee-zoo)* (P) map

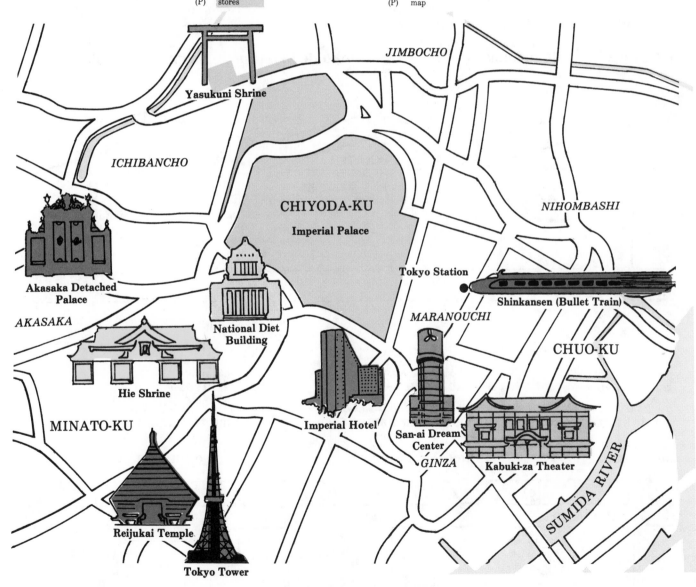

(tsoo-gee)   *(mee-seh)*
Tsugi no pēji de wa, there are all types of **Nihon no mise.** Be sure to fill in the blanks
following (P) on   (P) stores

e no shita with the **mise no namae.**
(P)   (P)

(pahn-yah)
Panya —
bakery
(pahn)   *(kye-mahss)*
Pan wa koko de kaimasu.
bread   here   at   one buys

(nee-koo-yah)
Nikuya —
butcher shop
(nee-koo)
Niku wa koko de kaimasu.
meat

(hah-nah-yah)
Hanaya —
florist
(hah-nah)
Hana wa koko de kaimasu.
flowers

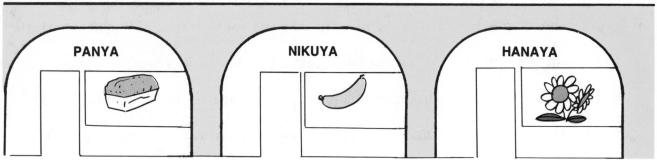

(kees-sah-ten)
Kissaten —
coffee shop/teahouse
(kōh-hēē)   *(noh-mee-mahss)*
Kōhii wa koko de nomimasu.
coffee   drink

(zahk-kah-ten)
Zakkaten —
general store
(den-chee)
Denchi wa koko de kaimasu.
battery

(yahk-kyoh-koo)
Yakkyoku —
drugstore
(ah-soo-pee-deen)
Asupirin wa koko de
aspirin

kaimasu.

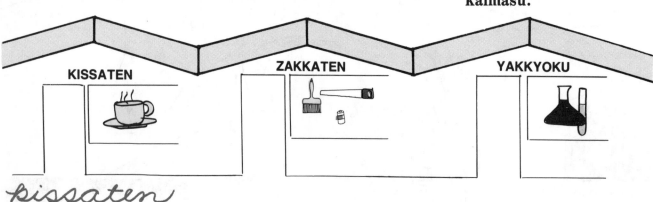

kissaten

(sen-tah-koo-yah)
Sentakuya —
laundry
(sen-tah-koo)
Sentaku wa koko de
laundry
(shee-mahss)
shimasu.
does

(tah-bah-koh-yah)
Tabakoya —
tobacco shop
(tah-bah-koh)·   *(hah-mah-kee)*
Tabako to hamaki wa
tobacco   and   cigars

koko de kaimasu.

(kah-shee-yah)
Kashiya —
candy store
(ah-meh)   *(choh-koh-dēh-toh)*
Ame to chokorēto wa
candy   and   chocolate

koko de kaimasu.

(gyōō-nyōō-ten)
Gyūnyūten —
dairy
(mee-doo-koo)   *(kye-mahss)*
Miruku wa koko de kaimasu.
milk   one buys

(kah-meh-dah-yah)
Kameraya —
camera store
(kah-meh-dah)
Kamera wa koko de
camera

kaimasu.

(yah-oy-yah)
Yaoya —
vegetable shop
(yah-sigh)
Yasai wa koko de kaimasu.
vegetables

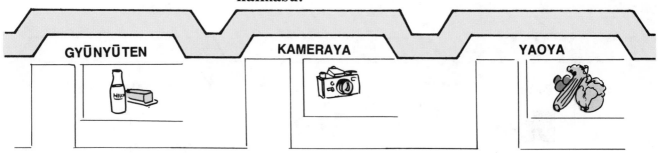

(chōō-shah-joh)
Chūshajo —
parking lot
(jee-dōh-shah)
Jidōsha wa koko de
car
(chōō-shah) (shee-mahss)
chūsha shimasu.
one parks

(dee-yōh-ten)
Riyōten —
barber shop
(sahn-pah-tsoo)
Sanpatsu wa koko de
haircut
(shee-mahss)
shimasu.
one does

(yōh-foo-koo-yah)
Yōfukuya —
tailor
(yōh-foo-koo)
Yōfuku wa koko de
clothes (Western-style)
(tsoo-koo-dee-mahss)
tsukurimasu.
one makes

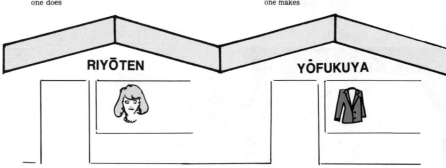

(yōō-bean-kyoh-koo)
Yūbinkyoku —
post office
(keet-teh)
Kitte wa koko de kaimasu.
stamps

(kay-sah-tsoo-choh)
Keisatsucho —
police station
(kay-kahn)
Keikan wa koko ni imasu.
police officer   in   is

(geen-kōh)
Ginkō —
bank
(dyōh-guy)
Ryōgae wa koko de shimasu.
money exchange

(shoh-koo-dyōh-heen-ten)
Shokuryōhinten —
grocery store
(nee-koo) (koo-dah-moh-noh)
Niku, kudamono to
meat   fruit   and
(mee-doo-koo)   *(kye-mahss)*
miruku wa koko de kaimasu.
milk   one buys

(hōh-seh-kee-ten)
Hōsekiten —
jewelry store
(hōh-seh-kee)
Hōseki wa koko
jewelry

de kaimasu.

(koo-dah-moh-noh-yah)
Kudamonoya —
fruit shop
(koo-dah-moh-noh)
Kudamono wa koko
fruit

de kaimasu.

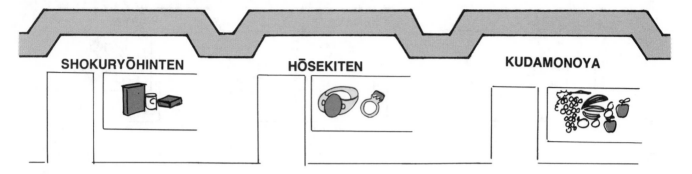

(ay-gah-kahn)
Eigakan —

(ay-gah)   *(mee-mahss)*
Eiga wa koko de mimasu.
movie   one sees

(sheen-boon-by-ten)
Shinbunbaiten —
newsstand
(sheen-boon)   *(zahsh-shee)*
Shinbun to zasshi wa koko
newspapers   and   magazines

de kaimasu.

(doh-die)   *(koo-dēē-neen-goo-yah)*
Dorai kuriininguya —
dry cleaner's
(doh-die)   *(koo-dēē-neen-goo)*
Dorai kuriiningu wa
dry cleaning
(shee-mahss)
koko de shimasu.
do

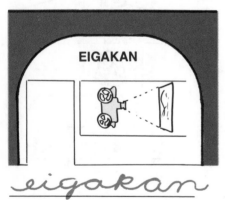

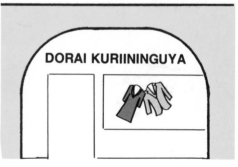

eigakan

(boon-bōh-goo-yah)
Bunbōguya —
stationery store
(kah-mee) (pen)   *(ehn-pee-tsoo)*
Kami, pen to enpitsu wa
paper   pens   pencils

koko de kaimasu.

(hohn-yah)
Honya —
bookstore
(hohn)
Hon wa koko de kaimasu.
books

(deh-pāh-toh)
Depāto —
department store
(nahn-deh-moh)
Koko de wa nandemo
everything

kaimasu (see Step 22).

(ee-chee-bah)
Ichiba —
market
(yah-sigh) *(koo-dah-moh-noh)*
Yasai to kudamono wa
vegetables and fruit

koko de kaimasu.

(sōō-pāh)
Sūpā —
supermarket
(nahn-deh-moh)
Koko de wa nandemo
everything

kaimasu.

(gah-soh-deen) *(soo-tahn-doh)*
Gasorin sutando —
gasoline   stand/station

Gasorin wa koko de

kaimasu.

(dyoh-kōh-shah)
Ryokōsha —
travel agency
(hee-kōh-kee) *(keep-poo)*
Hikōki no kippu
airplane   (P)   ticket

wa koko de kaimasu.

(toh-kay-yah)
Tokeiya —
clock/watchmaker's shop
(toh-kay)
Tokei wa koko de
clocks

kaimasu.

(sah-kah-nah-yah)
Sakanaya —
fish market
(sah-kah-nah)
Sakana wa koko de
fish

kaimasu.

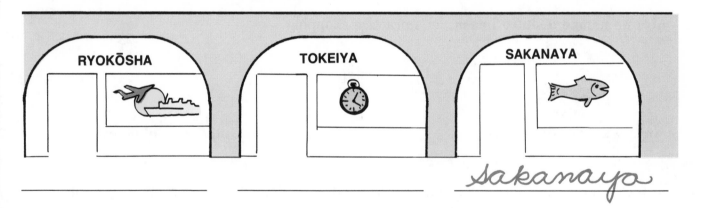

sakanaya

Tōkyō has four **shuyō no shotengai:** *(shoh-ten-guy)* **Ginza, Shibuya, Shinjuku to Ikebukuro.** *(geen-zah)* *(shee-boo-yah)* *(sheen-joo-koo)* *(ee-keh-boo-koo-doh)* Here,
major (P) shopping centers   and

anata wa will find large, **modan no depāto,** *(moh-dahn)* *(deh-pāh-toh)* containing a wide range of merchandise, as
modern (P) department stores

well as shopping arcades, specializing in traditional **Nihon no** goods. **Nihon no mise wa** *(mee-seh)*
(P)   (P) stores

itsu aite imasu ka? *(ee-tsoo)* *(eye-teh)* Most **mise** in **Nihon** are open **Getsuyōbi** *(geh-tsoo-yōh-bee)* through **Doyōbi, hachiji** *(doh-yōh-bee)* *(hah-chee-jee)*
when open   Monday   Saturday   eight o'clock

kara rokuji made. *(doh-koo-jee)* Some **mise,** however, are open **jūji kara hachiji made.** *(jōō-jee)* Also, some
six o'clock from   10 o'clock

mise in **shotengai** *(shoh-ten-guy)* are open on **Nichiyōbi.** *(nee-chee-yōh-bee)*
shopping centers   Sunday

Is there anything else that makes **Nihon no mise** *(mee-seh)* different from **Amerika no mise?** To
(P) stores   (P)

find out, look at the **e** *(eh)* on the following **pēji.**

97

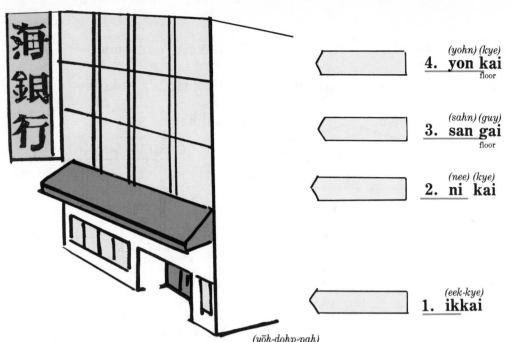

(yohn) (kye)
4. **yon kai**
floor

(sahn) (guy)
3. **san gai**
floor

(nee) (kye)
2. **ni kai**

(eek-kye)
1. **ikkai**

(yōh-dohp-pah)
What is called the ground floor in **Yōroppa** is called the first floor in **Nihon** (just like it is in

Amerika). In **Nihon,** food and **budōshu** are often located in the *(chee-kah)* **chika.** Notice that *(kye)* **kai** is
basement   floor

used with all **bangō** except **san,** which is used in combination with *(guy)* **gai.** **Ima anata wa**
floor

(mee-seh) *(sheet-teh) (ee-mahss)*
mise no namae o shitte imasu, let's practice shopping.
stores   (P)   know

> I. First step — *(doh-koh)* **Doko?**
> where

(pahn-yah)
Panya wa doko desu ka?
bakery

(geen-kōh)
Ginkō wa doko desu ka?
bank

Go through the *(mee-seh)* **mise** introduced in this Step and ask **"doko"** with each **mise.** Another

way of asking **"doko"** is to say

(pahn-yah) *(koh-noh) (chee-kah-koo)*
Panya wa kono chikaku desu ka?
bakery   here   near

(geen-kōh) *(koh-noh) (chee-kah-koo)*
Ginkō wa kono chikaku desu ka?
bank

Go through the **mise** again using this **atarashii shitsumon.**

> II. Next step — tell them what **anata wa** *(ee-dee-mahss)* **irimasu arui wa** *(hoh-shee) (dess)* **hoshii desu.**
> need   or   would like

1) Watashi wa _____ *(ee-dee-mahss)* **ga irimasu.**
need

2) Anata wa _____ *(moht-teh) (ee-mahss)* **o motte imasu ka?**
have

98   3) Watashi wa _____ *(hoh-shee) (dess)* **ga hoshii desu.**
would like

Watashi wa enpitsu ga irimasu.
(en-pee-tsoo) pencil *(ee-dee-mahss)* need

Watashi wa enpitsu ga hoshii desu.
(hoh-shēē)

Anata wa enpitsu o motte imasu ka?
(moht-teh) *(ee-mahss)* have

Watashi wa ringo ga irimasu.
(deen-goh) apples

Watashi wa ringo ga hoshii desu.

Anata wa ringo o motte imasu ka?

Go through the glossary at the back of **kono hon** and select **nijū no tango**. Drill the above
(nee-jōō) twenty (P)

patterns with **kono nijū no tango**. Don't cheat. Drill them **kyō**. **Ima** take **sara ni nijū no**
(P) *(kyōh)* today *(sah-dah)* more (P) (P)

tango from the glossary and do the same. **Ashita,** choose more **tango** and drill them also.
(ah-shtah) tomorrow

III.   Next step — find out "**ikura desu ka?**"
(ee-koo-dah) how much

Kore wa ikura desu ka? _____
(ee-koo-dah) how much

Enpitsu wa ikura desu ka?
(en-pee-tsoo) pencil *(ee-koo-dah)* how much

Hagaki wa ikura desu ka?

Kitte wa ikura desu ka?

Hon wa ikura desu ka?

Ringo wa ikura desu ka?
(deen-goh) apples

Orenji wa ikura desu ka?

Shinbun wa ikura desu ka?
(sheen-boon) newspaper

Pen wa ikura desu ka?

Using the same **tango** that **anata wa** selected **ue,** drill **kono shitsumon** also.
(oo-eh) above

IV.   If **anata wa** don't know where to find something, **anata wa iimasu**
(ēē-mahss) say

Asupirin wa doko de kaimasu ka?
(ah-soo-pee-deen) *(kye-mahss)* buy

Sangurasu wa doko de kaimasu ka?
(sahn-goo-dah-soo) sunglasses

Once **anata wa** find what **anata wa hoshii desu,** say
(hoh-shēē) would like *(dess)*

Kore ga hoshii desu. Dōmo.
(koh-deh) this *(dōh-moh)* thanks

Arui wa if **anata** would not like it,

Kore wa hoshiku arimasen. Dōmo.
(hoh-shee-koo)(ah-dee-mah-sen) would   not like

Anata wa ima are all set to shop for anything!

99

Step 22

(deh-pāh-toh)
Depāto
department store

At this point, **anata wa** should just about be ready for your **Nihon no ryokō**. *(dyoh-kōh)* Anata wa
(P) trip

have gone shopping for those last-minute odds 'n ends. Most likely, the **mise no** directory *(mee-seh)*
store (P)

at your local **depāto** *(deh-pāh-toh)* did not look like the one **shita**. *(shtah)* Already **anata wa takusan no tango** *(tah-koo-sahn)*
below many (P)

o shitte imasu *(sheet-teh) (ee-mahss)* and **anata** could guess at many others. **Anata wa** know that **"kodomo"** *(koh-doh-moh)* is
know

Nihongo for child, so if **anata wa irimasu** *(ee-dee-mahss)* something for a **kodomo, anata** would probably
need

look on the **san gai**, *(sahn) (guy)* wouldn't **anata?**
third floor

6. ■KAI	resutoran shokudo bāgen kōna shingu	kagami kagu jūtan	kaiga shashin denki seihin
5. ■KAI	hon terebi omocha	rajio gakki rekōdo kamera	bunbōgu zasshi shinbun
4. ■KAI	kuristaru hamono	daidokoroyōgu kagi	setomono tōki
3. ■GAI	kodomo hin fujin fuku fujin bōshi	shinshi fuku nyūyōji gutsu kotto	
2. ■KAI	kā akusesarii shitagi hankachi	mizugi fujin gutsu shinshi gutsu	supōtsu yōhin kōgu kyanpu yōhin
1. ■KAI	kasa chizu shinshi bōshi hōseki	tebukuro kawa seihin kutsushita beruto	tokei kōsui keshōhin
C. ■CHIKA	pan kissa sake, yōshu	shokuhin yasai, kudamono toriniku	reito shokuhin budōshu/wain niku

Let's start a checklist for **anata no ryokō**. Besides **fuku, nani ga irimasu ka?** *(foo-koo) (nah-nee) (ee-dee-mahss)* **Nani** do
clothing what need

100 **anata wa** need to take with **anata** to **Nihon?**

(pah-soo-pōh-toh)
pasupōto

(keep-poo)
kippu

(sōo-tsoo-kēh-soo)
sūtsukēsu

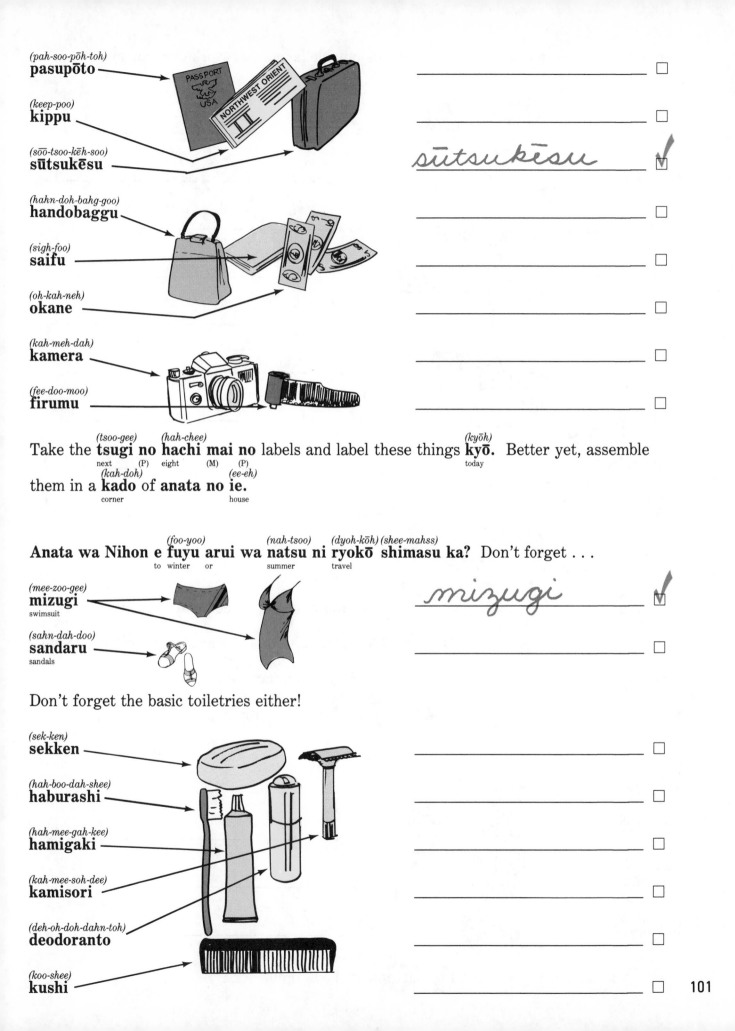

sūtsukēsu ✓

(hahn-doh-bahg-goo)
handobaggu

(sigh-foo)
saifu

(oh-kah-neh)
okane

(kah-meh-dah)
kamera

(fee-doo-moo)
firumu

Take the *(tsoo-gee)* **tsugi no** *(hah-chee)* **hachi mai no** labels and label these things **kyō.** *(kyōh)* today Better yet, assemble
next (P) eight (M) (P)
them in a **kado** of **anata no ie.**
(kah-doh) *(ee-eh)*
corner house

Anata wa Nihon e fuyu arui wa natsu ni ryokō shimasu ka? Don't forget . . .
(foo-yoo) *(nah-tsoo)* *(dyoh-kōh)* *(shee-mahss)*
to winter or summer travel

(mee-zoo-gee)
mizugi
swimsuit

mizugi ✓

(sahn-dah-doo)
sandaru
sandals

Don't forget the basic toiletries either!

(sek-ken)
sekken

(hah-boo-dah-shee)
haburashi

(hah-mee-gah-kee)
hamigaki

(kah-mee-soh-dee)
kamisori

(deh-oh-doh-dahn-toh)
deodoranto

(koo-shee)
kushi

For the rest of the **mono,** let's start with the outside layers and work our way in.

(ōh-bāh)
ōbā ————→ ☑

(dayn-kōh-toh)
reinkōto ————→ *reinkōto* ☐

(kah-sah)
kasa ————→ ☐

(teh-boo-koo-doh)
tebukuro ————→ ☐

(bōh-shee)
bōshi ———— ☐

(nah-gah-goo-tsoo)
nagagutsu ————→ ☐

(koo-tsoo)
kutsu ————→ *kutsu* ☐

(koo-tsoo-shtah)
kutsushita ————→ ☐

(pahn-tāy) *(soo-tohk-keen-goo)*
panteii sutokkingu ————→ ☑

(tsoo-gee) *(jōō-goh)*
Take the **tsugi no jūgo mai no** labels and label **kono mono.** Check and make sure that
next (P) fifteen (M) (P)

(kee-day)
they are **kirei** and ready for **anata no ryokō.** Be sure to do the same with the other **mono**
clean

*(nee-zoo-koo-dee)**(shee-mahss)* *(dee-stoh)*
that **anata wa nizukuri shimasu.** Check them off on **kono risuto** as **anata** organize
pack list

(hah-mee-gah-kee)
them. From **ima** on, **anata wa** have **"hamigaki"** and not "toothpaste."

(nye-toh-gown)
naitogaun ————→ ☐

(pah-jah-mah)
pajama ————→ ☐

(bah-soo-dōh-boo)
basurōbu ————→ ☐

(soo-deep-pah)
surippa ————→ ☐

(bah-soo-doh-boo) *(soo-deep-pah)* *(kye-gahn)*
Anata wa can also use **basurobu to surippa** at the **kaigan.**
and beach

102

(sōō-tsoo)
sūtsu _____ ☐

(neh-koo-tie)
nekutai _____ ☐

(hahn-kah-chee)
hankachi _____ ☐

(shah-tsoo)
shatsu _____ ☐

(jah-keh-tsoo)
jaketsu _____ ☐

(zoo-bohn)
zubon *zubon* ✓

(doh-deh-soo)
doresu _____ ☐

(boo-dow-soo)
burausu _____ ☐

(soo-kāh-toh)
sukāto _____ ☐

(sēh-tāh)
sētā _____ ☐

(boo-dah-jāh)
burajā _____ ☐

(soo-deep-poo)
surippu _____ ☐

(pahn-tāy)
panteii _____ ☐

(hah-dah-gee)
hadagi _____ ☐

Having assembled **kono mono, anata** are ready for **anata no ryokō.** However, being

human means occasionally forgetting something. Look again at the **depāto no** directory.
(deh-pāh-toh)
(P)

On what **kai** will **anata** find . . .
(kye)
floor

(sheen-shee) (foo-koo)
shinshi fuku? _____*San*_____ **gai de.**
gentlemen's clothing (guy) floor on

(foo-jeen) (bōh-shee)
fujin bōshi? _____ **gai de.**
women's hats

hon? _____ **kai de.**
(kye)
floor

(shee-tah-gee)
shitagi? _____ **kai de.** 103
lingerie

(koo-dee-stah-doo)
kuristaru?
crystal

_____ **kai de.**
(kye)
floor   on

(kōh-soo-ee)
kōsui?
perfume

_____ **kai de.**

(foo-jeen) (foo-koo)
fujin fuku?
women's   clothing

_____ **gai de.**
(guy)
floor

Be sure to remember your basic **shitsumon**. **Ima** repeat the **tsugi no kaiwa** out loud and
(tsoo-gee) *(kye-wah)*
following (P) conversation

repeat it again by filling in the blanks **shita.**
(shtah)

(foo-jeen) (foo-koo)
Fujin fuku wa doko desu ka? _____
women's   clothing

Fujin yōhin uriba desu. _____
(yōh-heen) (oo-dee-bah)
women's   wear   counter

Fujin yōhin uriba wa doko desu ka? _____
(oo-dee-bah)
counter

Ni kai desu. _____ *ni kai desu.* _____

Pan to budōshu wa doko desu ka? _____
and

Chika desu. _____
(chee-kah)
basement

Also don't forget to ask . . .

Erebētā wa doko desu ka? _____
(eh-deh-bēh-tāh)
elevator

Kaidan wa doko desu ka? _____
(kye-dahn)
stairs

Esukarētā wa doko desu ka? _____
(eh-skah-dēh-tāh)
escalator

Whether **anata wa** need **fujin fuku arui wa shinshi fuku, hitsuyō na tango wa** are
(foo-jeen) (foo-koo) *(sheen-shee)* *(hee-tsoo-yōh)*
women's   clothing or   gentlemen's   necessary (P)

the same. Practice your **atarashii shitsumon** with the **tsugi no fuku. Surippu wa doko**
(foo-koo) *(soo-deep-poo)*
(P) clothing   slip

desu ka?

104

And for some more **renshū** . . .

(foo-koo) (sigh-zoo) (foo-jeen)
Fuku no saizu: **FUJIN**
clothing (P) sizes   women

(nahn) (sigh-zoo)(dess) (kah)
Nan saizu desu ka?
what size is

_____

(koo-tsoo) (sigh-zoo)
Kutsu wa nan saizu desu ka?
shoes (P)   size

_____

(chōh-doh)
Chōdo desu.
just right

Chōdo desu.

(eye-mah-sen)
Aimasen.
does not fit

_____

(koh-deh) (ee-tah-dah-kee-mahss)
Kore o itadakimasu.
this   I take/receive

_____

(ee-koo-dah)
Ikura desu ka?
how much

_____

(soh-deh) (dah-keh) (dōh-moh) (ah-dee-gah-tōh)
Sore dake desu. **Dōmo arigatō.**
that only   thanks very much

_____

(koo-tsoo) **kutsu** shoes							
Amerika	5½	6	6½	7	7½	8	8½	9
Nihon	22½	23	23¾	24	24½	25	25½	25¾

(foo-koo) **fuku** clothing							
Amerika	4	6	8	10	12	14	16	18
Nihon	3	5	7	9	11	13	15	17

(boo-dow-soo) (sēh-tāh) **burausu, sētā** blouses sweater							
Amerika	4	6	8	10	12	14	16	18
Nihon	3	5	7	9	11	13	15	17

(sheen-shee)
Fuku no saizu: **SHINSHI**
gentlemen

kutsu					
Amerika	7½	8½	9½	10½	11½
Nihon	26	26¾	27¾	28	29

fuku							
Amerika	34	36	38	40	42	44	46
Nihon	S		M		L		LL

(shah-tsoo) **shatsu** shirts							
Amerika	14	14½	15	15½	16	16½	17	17½
Nihon	36	37	38	39	40	41	42	43

(joon-bee)
Ima anata wa have made all **anata no ryokō no junbi.** The next Step will give **anata** a
                                    (P) preparations

(mee-chee) (sign)
quick review of some of the pictogram **michi no sain** that **anata wa** will see in **Nihon.**
                                road (P) signs

(kōō-kōh)   (yoy)
Then **anata wa** are off to the **kūkō.** **Dōzo yoi ryokō o!**
                       airport   have a good trip

Step 23

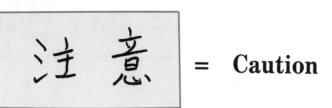 = **Caution**

Koko ni hijō ni taisetsu na Nihon no michi no sain ga arimasu. Don't forget that
(tie-seh-tsoo) *(mee-chee)* *(sign)*
here   very   important   (P)   (P)   road   (P)   signs

Nihonjin wa michi no hidari gawa ni unten shimasu. Dōzo yoi ryokō o!
(gah-wah) *(dōh-zoh)(yoy) (dyoh-kōh)*
(P)   side   (P)   have a good trip

(tah-noh-sheen-deh)
Tanoshinde kudasai!
have fun

一方通行

One-way

歩行者

Pedestrian crosswalk

停止

Stop

バス

Bus stop

タクシー

Taxi stand

駅

Station

地下鉄

Subway

案内所

Information center

警察署

Police station

営業中

Open

入口

Entrance

押ス

Push

休業中

Closed

出口

Exit

引ク

Pull

税関

Customs

免税

Duty-free

両替所

Money-exchange office

禁煙

No smoking

入浴禁止

No bathing

危険

Danger

予約

Reserved

行き止り

Dead end

GLOSSARY

A

ageta .... fried
aida .... between
aimasen .... it does not fit
airon .... iron
aisu kuriimu .... ice cream
aisu sukēto .... ice skating
aite imasu .... free, open
Ajia .... Asia
akai .... red
aki .... autumn
akemasu .... open
ame .... rain; candy
Amerika .... America
Amerikajin .... American
anata .... you
  anata no .... your
annaijo .... information desk
ano .... that over there
aoi .... blue
apāto .... apartment
araimasu .... wash
arigatō gozaimasu .... thank you
arimasu .... is, are
arui wa .... or
aruite .... on foot
asa .... morning
asagohan .... breakfast
ashita .... tomorrow
asupirin .... aspirin
atarashii .... new
atatakai .... warm
ate .... to
ato .... after
atsui .... hot; thick; cold

B

bā .... bar, cocktail lounge
ban .... evening
banana .... banana
bangō .... number
basu .... bus
basurobu .... bathrobe
bata .... butter
beddo .... bed
bēkon .... bacon
benri .... convenient
betsu .... separate
bifuteki .... beefsteak
biiru .... beer
bijutsukan .... art museum
binbō .... poor
bōru .... ball
bōshi .... hat
botan .... button
budōshu .... wine
Bukkyō .... Buddhism
bun .... part
bunboguya .... stationery store
burajā .... brassiere
burausu .... blouse
butaniku .... pork
byō .... second
byōin .... hospital
byōki .... sick

C

chairo .... brown
chakuriku shimasu .... land
chanoma .... tea room, dining room
chekku .... check
chichi .... father
chiisai .... small
chiizu .... cheese
chika .... basement
chikaku .... near
chikatetsu .... subway
chimu .... chime
chippu .... tip, gratuity
chizu .... map
cho .... block
chōdo .... just right
chokorēto .... chocolate
chōkyori .... long-distance
  chōkyori denwa ....
  .. long-distance/overseas telephone call
chōshoku .... breakfast
chotto .... just a minute
  Chotto! .... Say!
  chotto matte .... just wait
Chūgokugo .... Chinese
chūi .... warning
  chūi no chimu .... warning chime
chūmon shimasu .... order
chūsha shimasu .... park
chūshajo .... parking lot

D

dai .... charge
daidokoro .... kitchen
daigaku .... university
dake .... only
dare .... who
de .... and
de wa mata .... again (on telephone)
deguchi .... exit, main exit
dekimasu .... can make
demasu .... leave
denchi .... battery
denpō .... telegram
densha .... train
dentō .... light
denwa .... telephone, telephone call
  denwa bokusu .... telephone booth
  denwa chō .... telephone directory
  denwa kyoku .... telephone office
  denwa o kaketai desu ....
  ...... would like to make a telephone call
deodoranto .... deodorant
depāto .... department store
desu .... is, have
dezāto .... dessert
do .... how
dō itashimashite .... you're welcome
doa .... door
dōbutsuen .... zoo
Doitsu .... Germany
doko .... where
dōmo arigatō gozaimashita ....
  .... thank you very much
dono gurai .... how long
dorai kuriiningu .... dry cleaning
dorai kuriininguya .... dry cleaner's
doresu .... dress
dōri .... avenue
doru .... dollar
dōshi .... verb
dōshite .... why
Doyōbi .... Saturday
Dōzo yoi ryokō o! .... Have a good trip!

E

e .... picture; to
eiga .... movie
eigakan .... movie theater
Eigo .... English
eki .... train station
en .... yen
enjin .... engine
enpitsu .... pencil
erebētā .... elevator
esukarētā .... escalator

F

famiri .... family
firumu .... film
fōku .... fork
fujin .... woman, women
  fujin fuku .... women's clothing
  fujin yōhin .... women's wear
Fujisan .... Mt. Fuji
fukimasu .... blow
fuku .... clothes, clothing
fun .... minutes
funshitsu .... lost (articles)
Furansu .... France
Furansugo .... French
furimasu .... fall
furoba .... bathroom, bathing room
furūtsu .... fruit
  furūtsu jūsu .... fruit juice
  furūtsu sarada .... fruit salad
futsū ressha .... local, ordinary train
futsuka .... second
futtō .... boil
futtobōru .... football
fuyu .... winter

G

ga .... but
gaido .... guide
gaikoku .... foreign country
  gaikoku no .... foreign
gakkō .... school
garēji .... garage
garō .... art gallery
gasorin .... gasoline
  gasorin sutando .... gasoline station
gasu rēnji .... gas range
geki .... play (theater)
gekijō .... theater
gēmu .... game
genkan .... main entrance
gēto .... gate
Getsuyōbi .... Monday
ginkō .... bank
go .... five
gochisōsama .... delicious
Gogatsu .... May
gogo .... afternoon
gohan .... rice
gohyaku .... five hundred
gojū .... fifty
gōkei .... total
gomibako .... wastepaper basket
gosen .... five thousand
guramu .... gram
gurasu .... glass
gurūpu .... group
gyokairui .... fish and seafood dish
gyūniku .... beef
gyūnyūten .... dairy

H

haburashi .... toothbrush
hachi .... eight
Hachigatsu .... August
hachijū .... eighty
hadagi .... undershirt
hagaki .... postcard
haha .... mother
hai .... yes
haiiro .... gray
hairimasu .... enter
hajimarimasu .... begin

hakubutsukan .... museum
hamaki .... cigar
hamigaki .... toothpaste
hamu egguzu .... ham and eggs
hana .... flower
hanashichū .... the line is busy
hanashimasu .... speak
hanaya .... florist
hanbāgu .... hamburger
handobaggu .... handbag
hankachi .... handkerchief
haraimasu .... pay
haru .... spring
hashi .... chopsticks
hayai .... fast
heijitsu .... weekday
heinetsu ..... normal (body) temperature
herikoputā .... helicopter
heya .... room
hi .... day
hidari .... left
    hidari ni .... to the left
higashi .... east
    higashi no .... eastern
hijō deguchi ....emergency exit
hijō ni .... very
hikari .... express bullet train
hikōki .... airplane
hikui .... low
hirugohan .... lunch
hiruma .... daytime, midday
hito .... person
hitobito .... people
hitsuyō .... necessary
hōkō .... direction
hōmu .... platform
hon .... book
honya .... bookstore
hōseki .... jewelry
hōsekiten .... jewelry store
hoshii desu .... would like
hoshiku arimasen ...... would not like
hosuteru .... hostel
hoteru .... hotel
hotto doggu .... hot dog
hyaku .... one hundred

I

ichi .... one
ichiba .... market
Ichigatsu .... January
ichiman .... ten thousand
ie .... house
Igirisu .... England
ii .... good, nice
iie .... no
iimasu .... say
ikaga .... how
ikimasu .... go
ikitai desu .... would like to go
iku .... go
ikura .... how much
ikutsu .... how many
ima .... living room; now
imasen .... am not
imasu .... is, are
inchi .... inch
Ingurando .... England
inki .... ink
intabyū .... interview
inu .... dog
ippai .... one glass
ippanteki .... typical
irasshaimase .... welcome
irasshaimasu .... is in
iremasu .... insert
iri tamago .... scrambled eggs
iriguchi .... entrance

irimasu .... need
iro .... color
isha .... doctor
isu .... chair
itadakimasu .... take, receive;
                I will receive the food
itameta .... fried
Itaria .... Italy
Itariago .... Italian
itsu .... when
itsuka .... fifth
ittō .... first-class

J

jaketsu .... jacket
jamu .... jam
jerii .... jelly
jettoki .... jet airplane
jibiki .... dictionary
jidōsha .... car
jikan .... time
jikoku .... time
jikokuhyo .... schedule, timetable
jinja .... shrine
jinjāeru .... ginger ale
jisoku .... per hour
jitensha .... bicycle
jōhō .... information
jū .... ten
jūdan shimasu .... traverse
Jūgatsu .... October
jūgo .... fifteen
jūgofun .... quarter, 15 minutes
    jūgofun mae .... quarter before
    jūgofun sugi .... quarter after
jugyō .... lesson
jūhachi .... eighteen
jūichi .... eleven
Jūichigatsu .... November
jūku .... nineteen
jūkyū .... nineteen
jūnana .... seventeen
junbi .... preparation
jūni .... twelve
Jūnigatsu .... December
junkyū .... ordinary train
jūroku .... sixteen
jūsan .... thirteen
jūshi .... fourteen
jūshichi .... seventeen
jūsu .... juice
jūyon .... fourteen

K

kabe .... wall
kado .... corner
kagami .... mirror
kai .... floor
kaidan .... stairs
kaigan .... beach
kaimasu .... buy
kaiwa .... conversation
kakarimasu ...... take (time); hang
kakebuton .... quilt
kaketai desu ...... would like to make
kakimasu .... write
kamera .... camera
kami .... paper
kamisori .... razor
kanemochi .... rich
kani .... crab
kanjōgaki .... bill
kanojo .... she
kāpetto .... carpet
kara .... from
kare .... he
karendā .... calendar
karera .... they

kasa .... umbrella
Kashi .... Fahrenheit
kashiya .... candy store
katamichi .... one-way
kāten .... curtain
Katorikku .... Catholicism
katteguchi .... side entrance
Kayōbi .... Tuesday
kaze .... wind
kazoku .... family
keikan .... police officer
keisatsucho .... police station
kekko .... fine
kenkō .... healthy
kesa .... this morning
kiiroi .... yellow
kimasu .... come
Kin'en desu ka? ... Is smoking prohibited?
kinō .... yesterday
Kinyōbi .... Friday
kion .... temperature
kippu .... ticket
    kippu kiri .... ticket collector
kirei .... clean
kiri .... fog
kiro .... kilometer
kissaten ...... coffee shop, teahouse
kita .... north
    kita no .... northern
kitsuensha ...... smoking compartment
kitte .... stamp
kōcha .... black tea
kodama .... ordinary bullet train
kodomo .... child, children
kōen .... park
kōhii .... coffee
kōka .... coin
koko .... here
kōkūbin .... airmail
kokunai .... domestic
kokusai .... international
Kokusai Denwa Denden Kosha ......
    International Telephone and
            Telegraph Office
konban wa .... good evening
konnichi wa .... good day, hello
kono .... this, these
konsāto .... concert
koppu .... cup
kore .... this
koshō .... pepper
kōshū .... public
kōsoku dōro .... freeway
kōsui .... perfume
kotae .... answer
kōtsū kippu ....traffic ticket
koushiniku .... veal
kozutsumi .... package
ku .... nine
kudamono .... fruit
kudamonoya .... fruit shop
kudasai .... please; please give me
Kugatsu .... September
kūkō .... airport
kurikaeshimasu .... repeat
kuristaru .... crystal
kuroi .... black
kurossuwādo ...... crossword puzzle
kusa .... grass
kyōkai .... church
kyū .... nine
kyujū .... ninety
kyūka .... holiday
kyūkō ressha .... express train
kushi .... comb
kutsu .... shoe
kutsushita .... sock
kyabarē ...... bar, cocktail lounge
kyō .... today **109**

M

machiaishitsu	waiting room
machinē	matineé
made	to
mado	window
mae	in front of
magarimasu	turn
māgarin	margarine
mairu	mile
māketto	market
makura	pillow
māmarēdo	marmalade
man	ten thousand
manējā	manager
manekin	mannequin
maruku	mark
masāji	massage
massugu	straight ahead
masukotto	mascot
mata dōzo	please come again
matte	wait
matte imasu	wait for
mawashimasu	dial
medama yaki tamago	fried egg
megane	eyeglasses
menrui	noodle dishes
menyū	menu
meron	melon
messēji	message
mētoru	meter
mezamashi dokei	alarm clock
michi	road, street
michi no sain	road sign
midori	green
migi	right
migi ni	to the right
mijikai	short
mimasu	see
minami	south
minami no	southern
miruku	milk
mise	store
misemasu	show
misete	show
mite	look
miyako	capital
mizu	water
mizugi	swimsuit
mo	also
mō	more; already
mō ichido	once more
modan	modern
modorimasu	return
Mokuyōbi	Thursday
momoiro	pink
mondai	problem
mono	thing
monorēru	monorail
moshi, moshi	hello
mōshimasu	speaking
mōtā	motor
motte imasu	have
motto	more
motto chiisai	smaller
mushita	steamed
musuko	son
musume	daughter

N

nagagutsu	boot
nagai	long
naifu	knife
naitogaun	nightgown
naka	inside
namae	name
namamono	raw
nan	what
nanajū	seventy
nandemo	everything
nani	what
nanimo	nothing
nanji	what time
Nanji desu ka?	What time is it?
nanji ni?	at what time?
napukin	napkin
naraimasu	learn
natsu	summer
naze	why
nedan	price
nekkuresu	necklace
neko	cat
nekutai	necktie
nemasu	sleep
ni	two
ni	in, into, at, on
nibanme	second
nichi	day
Nichiyōbi	Sunday
Nigatsu	February
Nihon	Japan
Nihongo	Japanese language
Nihonjin	Japanese
nijū	twenty
niku	meat
niku ryōri	meat dish
nikuya	butcher shop
nishi	west
nishi no	western
nita	cooked
nitemasu	similar
nitō	second-class
niwa	garden
nizukuri shimasu	pack
nokotta	remaining
nomimasu	drink
nomimono	beverage
norikaemasu	transfer (vehicles)
norimasu	ride; board

O

oba	aunt
ōbā	overcoat
obasan	grandmother
ōbāshūzu	overshoes
ocha	tea
ōdā	order
odoburu	hors d'oeuvre
ōfuku	round-trip
ofuro	bath
ohayō gozaimasu	good morning
ojiisan	grandfather
ojisan	uncle
okane	money
okāsan	mother
okashi	sweet cake
ōkē	okay
ōkii	big
ōku	a lot
okurete imasu	late
okurimasu	send
omiyage	souvenir
omoshiroi	interesting
omuretsu	omelette
onna no hito	woman
onna no hitotachi	women
onna no kyōdai	sister
onsu	ounce
orenji	orange
orenji jūsu	orange juice
orimasu	disembark, get out
orugan	organ
osara	plate
Oshokuji o dōzo!	Enjoy your meal!
osoi	slow
otera	temple
otoko no hito	man

otoko no hitotachi	men
otoko no kyōdai	brother
otomodachi	friend
otōsan	father
otsuri	change (money)
owatta	finished
oyasuminasai	good night

P

pai	pie
pajama	pajamas
pan	bread
pankēki	pancake
panteii	underpants
panteii sutokkingu	pantyhose
pantsu	pants
panya	bakery
pāsento	percent
pasu	pass, free ticket
pasupōtō	passport
pēji	page
pen	pen
pondo	pound
pōtā	porter
pūru	pool, swimming pool

R

rajio	radio
ranpu	lamp
rasshiawā	rush hour
referii	referee
reinkōto	raincoat
reizōko	refrigerator
remon	lemon
renshū	practice
renta kā	rental car
renta kā ya	rental car agency
reshiiba	telephone receiver
resutoran	restaurant
ringo	apple
rippa	excellent
risuto	list
rittoru	liter
riyōten	barber shop
robii	lobby
roku	six
Rokugatsu	June
rokujū	sixty
rōru pan	bread roll
Roshiago	Russian
ryōgae	money exchange
ryokan	inn
ryōkin	fare
ryokō	journey, trip
ryokō shimasu	travel
ryokōsha	tourist, traveler, travel agency
ryōriya	restaurant serving Japanese food
ryōshin	parents
ryōshūsho	receipt
ryōtei	restaurant serving Japanese food

S

sābisu	service
sagashimasu	look for
saidā	cider
saifu	wallet
sain	sign, signature
saizu	size
saji	spoon
sakana	fish
sakanaya	fish market
sake	rice wine
samui	cold
san	three; honorable, Mr.
sanbanme	third
sandaru	sandal
sandoicchi	sandwich

Sangatsu .... March
sangurasu .... sunglasses
sanjū .... thirty
sanpatsu .... haircut
sarada .... salad
sashimi .... raw fish
satsu .... bill, currency
sayonara .... goodbye
sei ga hikui .... short
sei ga takai .... tall
seiten .... fair
seki .... seat
sekken .... soap
sen ..... one thousand; track; subway line
senmendai .... washstand
senpō barai .... collect call
sentaku .... laundry
sentakuya .... laundry
Sesshi .... Centigrade
sētā .... sweater
shako .... garage
shampen .... champagne
shatsu .... shirt
shawā .... shower
shi .... four
shichi .... seven
Shichigatsu .... July
Shigatsu .... April
shigoto .... work
shimarimasu .... closed
shimasu .... do
shinai .... local
   shinai denwa ..... local telephone call
shinbun .... newspaper
shinbunbaiten .... newsstand
shindaisha .... sleeping car
shinkansen .... bullet train
Shinkyō .... Protestantism
shinnyū kinshi .... do not enter
shinseki .... relative
shinshi .... gentleman, gentlemen
   shinshi fuku .... gentlemen's clothing
shinshitsu .... bedroom
Shintō .... Shintoism
shio .... salt
   shio mizu .... salt water
shiroi .... white
shirumono ...... Japanese-style soup
shisutemu .... system
shita .... under, below
shitagi .... lingerie
shitsurei .... excuse me
shitsumon .... question
shitte imasu .... know
shizuka ni .... quietly
shokkidana .... cupboard
shokubutsuen .... botanical gardens
shokudo .... dining room
shokudōsha .... dining car
shokuji .... meal
shokuryōhinten .... grocery store
shosai .... study
shotengai .... shopping center
shūkan .... week; custom
shūkyō .... religion
shuppatsu .... departure
soba .... noodles
sobaya .... noodle shop
sofā .... sofa
sofubo .... grandparent
soko .... there
sono .... that, those
sore .... that
sore kara .... and then; then
subete .... everything
   subete no mono .... everything
suchuwādesu .... stewardess
Suiyōbi .... Wednesday
sukejūru .... schedule

sukii .... ski
sukoshi .... a little
sumimasen .... sorry (to bother you)
sunakku .... bar, cocktail lounge
sunde imasu .... live
sūpā .... supermarket
Supein .... Spain
sūpu .... Western-style soup
surippa .... slipper
surippu .... underslip
sushi .... vinegared rice and fish
sushi ya .... restaurant that serves
                   sashimi and sushi
sutēki .... steak
sūtsu .... suit
sūtsukēsu .... suitcase
suzushii .... cool

T

tabako .... tobacco
tabakoya .... tobacco store
tabemasu .... eat
tadashii .... correct
taisetsu .... important
taiya .... tire
taizai shimasu .... stay
takai .... high; expensive
takusan .... a lot, many
takushii .... taxi
   takushii noriba .... taxi stand
tamago .... egg
   tamago ryōri .... egg dish
tango .... word
Tanoshinde kudasai! .... Have fun!
taoru .... towel
tashoku .... multicolored
tatami .... straw mat
tatoeba .... for example
tatta .... only
te .... hand
tebukuro .... glove
tēburu .... table
tegami .... letter
teikoku .... imperial
teiryūjo .... bus stop, subway stop
tempura .. deep-fried fish and vegetables
tenjō .... ceiling
tenki .... weather
tenrankaijo .... exhibition hall
tenugui .... handtowel
terebi .... t.v.
terebijon .... television
tobimasu .... fly
tōchaku .... arrival
toire .... lavatory, toilet
tokei .... clock
tokeiya .... clock and watchmaker's shop
tokkyū ressha ..... special express train
tokushoku .... special
tomodachi .... friend
tonari .... next to
tonkatsu .... pork cutlet
toriniku .... poultry
toritsugi .... connection
torofii .... trophy
toshi .... year; city
toshiyori .... old
toshokan .... library
tosuto .... toast
tsugi .... next
tsukatte imasu .... being used, occupied
tsukemono .... pickled vegetables
tsukemono ni shita .... pickled
tsuki .... month
tsukimasu .... arrive
tsukue .... desk
tsukurimasu .... make
tsumetai .... cold

tsūwa .... telephone call
tsuzukeraremasu .... continue
tsuki .... month

U

udon .... noodles
udonya .... noodle shop
ue .... over, above, on top
uētā .... waiter
uētoresu .... waitress
uketsuke .... counter, front desk
unten shimasu .... drive
untenshu .... driver
unyusho .... transportation
uriba .... counter
urimasu .... sell
ushinaimasu .... lose
ushiro .... behind
usui .... thin

W

wagaya .... our home
wakai .... young
wakarimasu .... understand
warui .... bad
watashi I
watashitachi .... we

Y

yaita .... baked, grilled
yakamashiku .... loudly
yakkyoku .... drugstore
yama .... mountain
yaoya .... vegetable shop
yasai .... vegetable
yasui .... inexpensive
yobarete imasu .... be called
yōbi .... day of the week
yobirin .... doorbell
yōfuku .... Western-styled clothes
yōfuku dansu .... clothes closet
yōfukuya .... tailor
yōgashi .... pastry
yōgashiya .... pastry shop
yoku .... much
yomimasu .... read
yon .... four
yonjū .... forty
Yōroppa .... Europe
yoru .... night
yoyaku .... reservation
yoyaku shimasu .... reserve, book
yuagari taoru .... bathtowel
yūbin .... mail
yūbinbako .... mailbox
yūbinkyoku .... post office
yudeta .... boiled
yūhan .... dinner
yukata .... cotton robe
yuki .... snow; to
yukisaki .... destination
yukkuri .... slowly

Z

zakkaten .... general store
zasshi .... magazine
zeikin .... tax
zenbu .... everything
zensai .... appetizer
zero .... zero
zō .... elephant
zubon .... trousers

111

DRINKING GUIDE

This drinking guide is intended to explain the variety of beverages available to you in Japan. It is by no means complete. Some of the experimenting has been left up to you, but this should get you started. The asterisks (*) indicate brand names.

BIIRU (beer)

BIIRU (beer) **Biiru** is available by the bottle or on draught. Both imported and domestic **biiru** are served in **Nihon**. **Nihon no biiru** has a distinctive taste, somewhat like English lager.

*Sapporo
*Asahi
*Suntory
*Kirin

BUDŌSHU/WAIN (wine)

BUDŌSHU/WAIN (wine) **Budōshu** can be purchased by the **gurasu** or by the **bin** (bottle). Most **budōshu** is imported from France and Italy.

sake	rice wine

Sake is a traditional **Nihon no** drink, brewed from rice. It is served warm in porcelain cups and goes well with **Nihon no** food.

umeshu	plum wine
shiroi wain	white wine
akai wain	red wine
rōze wain	rosé wine
shampen	champagne

OCHA (tea)

hōji cha	green tea
gyokurō	green tea
kōcha	black tea
ban cha	brown tea
genmai cha	popped-rice tea

ARUKŌRU INRYŌ (alcoholic beverages/spirits)

ARUKŌRU INRYŌ (alcoholic beverages/spirits) Both imported and domestic **arukōru inryō** are available in **Nihon**.

uisuki	whisky
*Suntory	
*Nikka	
*Ocean	
haiboru	whisky and soda
uokka	vodka
sukuryū doraibā	screwdriver
ramu	rum
jin	gin
jin tonikku	gin and tonic
burandē	brandy
konnyakku	cognac
sherii	sherry
pōtowain	port
saidā	cider
berumotto	vermouth
rikyūru	liqueur
aperitifu	aperitif

HOKA NO NOMIMONO (other beverages)

kōhii	coffee (strong)
Amerikan kohii	American coffee (mild)
ekkusupuresso kohii	espresso coffee
kuriimu iri kohii	coffee with cream
furūtsu jūsu	fruit juice
orenji jūsu	orange juice
painappuru jūsu	pineapple juice
gurēpu jūsu	grape juice
tomato jūsu	tomato juice
Koka Kōra	Coca-Cola
Pepushi Kōra	Pepsi-Cola
Fuantā	Fanta
jinjaēru	ginger ale
remonādo	lemonade
mineraru uōtā	mineral water
tonikku uōtā	tonic water
sōdāsui	soda water
miruku	milk
miruku sēki	milk shake
hotto chokorēto	hot chocolate
kokoa	cocoa

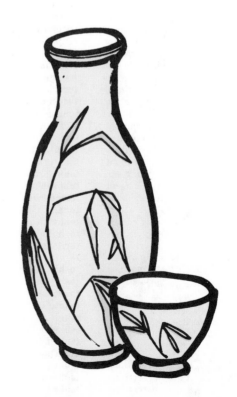

Menyū
menu

Otsumami/Ōdoburu (hors d'oeuvres)

kani	crab
ika	cuttlefish/squid
ika no shiokara	salted cuttlefish guts
kanisu	vinegared crab
kaiso moriawase	selected seaweed
nishin	herring
kunsei no nishin	smoked herring
maguro	tuna
ebi	shrimp
hamaguri	clams

Shirumono/Sūpu (soup)

akadashi	red-bean paste soup
misoshiru	white-bean paste soup
suimono/sumashijiru	clear soup
oden	vegetable and fish-paste stew

Tamago Ryōri (egg dishes)

tamagoyaki/omuretsu	omelette
okonomiyaki	meat-and-vegetable omelette
tamagodōfu	egg custard
tamago sandoicchi	egg sandwich
medama yaki	fried egg
yude tamago	hard-boiled egg
hanne tamago	soft-boiled egg
iritamago	scrambled eggs
chawan mushi	cup-steamed egg custard

Sunakku (snacks)

kēki	cake
ita chokorēto	chocolate bar

---

aisu kuriimu	ice cream
okashi/yōgashi	pastry
pai	pie
wagashi	sweet cakes
mitsumame	red beans and gelatin
zenzai	red beans and pounded rice
kudamono	fruit

Kudamono/Furūtsu (fruit)

nashi	pear
budō	grapes
mikan	tangerine
meron	melon
ringo	apple
remon	lemon
banana	banana
orenji	orange
painappuru	pineapple
suika	watermelon
momo	peach
gurepu furūtsu	grapefruit
kaki	persimmon
ichigo	strawberries
puramu	plum
ume maki	pickled plum
furūtsu sarada	fruit salad

Nomimono (beverages)

ocha	green tea
kōcha	black tea
kōhii	coffee
miruku	milk
jūsu	juice
Koka Kōra	Coca-Cola
jinjāēru	ginger ale
mineraru uōtā	mineral water
sake	rice wine
biiru	beer
budōshu/wain	wine

Tsukurikata (ways of preparation)

namamono ni shita	raw
tsukemono ni shita	pickled
yudeta	boiled
mushita	steamed
yaita	baked/grilled
ageta/itameta	fried
nita	cooked

Ippan (general)

tōfu	beancurd
shōyu	soy sauce
shio	salt
koshō	pepper
satō	sugar
abura	oil
su	vinegar
bata	butter
māgārin	margarine
gohan	rice
udon/soba	noodles
pan	bread
sandoicchi	sandwich
jamu	jam
jerii	jelly
chiizu	cheese
kechappu	ketchup
karashi	mustard

Oshokuji o dōzo!

Yasai (vegetables)

tsukemono	pickled vegetables
hasu	lotus root
daikon	white radish
tororoimo	grated yam
shiso	beefsteak plant
moyashi	bean sprouts
kyabetsu	cabbage
hakusai	Chinese cabbage
tororoimo	taro root
hōrensō	spinach
ninjin	carrots
kyūri	cucumber
ninniku	garlic
negi	leeks/green onions
tamanegi	dried onion
retasu	lettuce
tomato	tomato
piman	green pepper
shiitake	mushrooms
nasu	eggplant
asuparagasu	asparagus

Niku Ryōri (meat dishes)

Gyūniku (beef)

bifu kare raisu	beef and curried rice
sukiyaki	beef and vegetables in soy sauce
shabu shabu	beef and vegetables in seasoned broth
teppan yaki	meat and vegetables cooked on iron grill
hanbāga	hamburger
bifuteki	beefsteak
sāroin	sirloin
hireniku	filet mignon
rōsuto bifu	roast beef
bifu shichū	beef stew

Butaniku (pork)

tonkatsu	pork cutlet
sōsēji	sausage
hamu	ham
buta no kakuni	stewed, cubed pork
hotto doggu	hot dog

Toriniku (chicken)

yakitori	barbecued chicken on skewers
rōsuto chikin	roast chicken
tori no karāge	fried chicken

Gyokai Ryōri (fish and seafood dishes)

sashimi	sliced raw fish (usually tuna)
maguro	tuna
katsuo	bonito
aji	pompano
saba	mackerel
tako	octopus
awabi	abalone
ebi	shrimp
hirame	flat fish
tai	sea bream
kohada	gizzard shad
ikura	salmon roe
kani	crab
hotategai/kaibashira	scallops
tarako	cod roe
kazunoko	herring roe
anago	conger eel
ika	cuttlefish/squid
kisu	smelt
uni	raw sea urchin
aoyagi	round clam
hamachi	young yellowtail
mirugai	surf clam
ise ebi	lobster
unagi	eel
iwashi	sardine
kaki	oyster
kamasu	pike
karei	turbot
sake	salmon
tara	cod
nishin	herring
nishin no kunsei	kippered herring
masu	trout
moriawase	selected seafood
koi no arai	sliced raw carp
fugusashi	sliced globefish
ebi furai	fried shrimp
wakasagi no furai	fried smelt
kabayaki	fish dipped in soy sauce
mushi awabi	steamed abalone
saba no misoni	stewed mackerel with soybean paste
yaki hamaguri	broiled clams
sakana yaki	broiled fish
sushi	vinegared fish and rice
nigirizushi	hand-pressed rice ball sushi
chirashizushi	vinegared pilaf-style rice with egg and vegetables
makizushi	fish and rice rolled in seaweed
inarizushi	vinegared rice wrapped in seaweed
tekka maki	tuna wrapped in seaweed and rice
kappa maki	cucumber wrapped in seaweed and rice
takuan maki	pickled white radish wrapped in seaweed and rice
norimaki	sushi wrapped in seaweed
tempura	deep-fried fish and vegetables

Udon/Soba (noodles)

tempura udon	noodles with deep-fried prawns and vegetables
kitsune udon	noodles with fried beancurd
nabeyaki udon	seafood and fish cakes in hot broth
tsukimi udon	noodles with raw egg
tamago toji udon	noodles with egg
tanuki udon	noodles with tempura batter
yakisoba	sauced noodles tossed with cabbage and other vegetables
kake soba	noodles served in broth
tororo soba	noodles with yam paste
supagetti	spaghetti

Gohan (rice)

tendon	shrimp and vegetable tempura over rice
unadon	eel over rice
katsudon	pork cutlet over rice
oyakodon	chicken over rice
tamagodon	egg over rice
omu raisu	rice omelette
pirafu	rice pilaf

(koo-dah-sigh)
kudasai

(moht-teh) *(ee-mahss)*
motte imasu

(dess)
desu

(ee-mahss)
imasu

(hah-nah-shee-mahss)
hanashimasu

(kye-mahss)
kaimasu

(tie-zye) *(shee-mahss)*
taizai shimasu

(chōō-mohn) *(shee-mahss)*
chūmon shimasu

(soon-deh) *(ee-mahss)*
sunde imasu

(yoh-bah-deh-teh) *(ee-mahss)*
yobarete imasu

(kee-mahss)
kimasu

(ee-kee-mahss)
ikimasu

have	please (give me)
is	is
buy	speak
order	stay
be called	live
go	come

(nah-die-mahss) **naraimasu**	*(ee-dee-mahss)* **irimasu**
(hoh-shēē) *(dess)* **hoshii desu**	*(ēē-mahss)* **iimasu**
(tah-beh-mahss) **tabemasu**	*(noh-mee-mahss)* **nomimasu**
(ah-dee-mahss) **arimasu**	*(maht-teh)* *(ee-mahss)* **matte imasu**
(wah-kah-dee-mahss) **wakarimasu**	*(oo-dee-mahss)* **urimasu**
(koo-dee-kah-eh-shee-mahss) **kurikaeshimasu**	*(mee-mahss)* **mimasu**

need	learn
say	would like
drink	eat
wait for	is
sell	understand
see	repeat

(oh-koo-dee-mahss) **okurimasu**	*(neh-mahss)* **nemasu**
(sah-gah-shee-mahss) **sagashimasu**	*(shee-mahss)* **shimasu**
(kah-kee-mahss) **kakimasu**	*(mee-seh-mahss)* **misemasu**
(hah-die-mahss) **haraimasu**	*(sheet-teh)* *(ee-mahss)* **shitte imasu**
(noh-dee-mahss) **norimasu**	*(dyoh-kōh)* *(shee-mahss)* **ryokō shimasu**
(yoh-mee-mahss) **yomimasu**	*(toh-bee-mahss)* **tobimasu**

sleep	send
do	look for
show	write
know	pay
travel	ride
fly	read

(chah-koo-dee-koo)   *(shee-mahss)*

chakuriku shimasu

(yoy-yah-koo)   *(shee-mahss)*

yoyaku shimasu

(tsoo-kee-mahss)

tsukimasu

(deh-mahss)

demasu

(oon-ten)   *(shee-mahss)*

unten shimasu

(noh-dee-mahss)

norimasu

(oh-dee-mahss)

orimasu

(noh-dee-kah-eh-mahss)

norikaemasu

(ah-die-mahss)

araimasu

(oo-shee-nye-mahss)

ushinaimasu

(kah-kah-dee-mahss)

kakarimasu

(hah-tah-dah-kee-mahss)

hatarakimasu

reserve/book	land
leave	arrive
board	drive
transfer (vehicles)	disembark/get out
lose	wash
work	take (time)

(nee-zoo-koo-dee)   *(shee-mahss)*

nizukuri shimasu

(kōh-kahn)   *(shee-mahss)*

kōkan shimasu

(ah-kee-mahss)

akimasu

(shee-meh-mahss)

shimemasu

(dyoh-dee)   *(shee-mahss)*

ryori shimasu

(hah-jee-mah-dee-mahss)

hajimarimasu

(ah-meh)   *(gah)*   *(foo-dee-mahss)*

Ame ga furimasu.

(yoo-kee)   *(gah)*   *(foo-dee-mahss)*

Yuki ga furimasu.

(kee-dee)   *(gah)*   *(kah-kah-dee-mahss)*

Kiri ga kakarimasu.

(kah-zeh)   *(gah)*   *(foo-kee-mahss)*

Kaze ga fukimasu.

(byōh-kee)   *(ken-kōh)*

byōki - kenkō

(ēē)   *(wah-doo-ee)*

ii - warui

exchange (money)   pack

close   open

begin   cook

It snows.   It rains.

It is windy.   It is foggy.

good - bad   sick - healthy

atsui - tsumetai
(ah-tsee) *(tsoo-meh-tie)*

shizuka ni -
(shee-zoo-kah) *(nee)*
yakamashiku
(yah-kah-mah-shee-koo)

mijikai - nagai
(mee-jee-kye) *(nah-guy)*

sei ga takai -
(say) *(gah)* *(tah-kye)*
sei ga hikui
(say) *(gah)* *(hee-koo-ee)*

atsui - usui
(ah-tsee) *(oo-soo-ee)*

hayai - osoi
(hi-yi) *(oh-soy)*

ue - shita
(oo-eh) *(shtah)*

hidari - migi
(hee-dah-dee) *(mee-gee)*

takai - hikui
(tah-kye) *(hee-koo-ee)*

toshiyori - wakai
(toh-shee-yoh-dee) *(wah-kye)*

yasui - takai
(yah-soo-ee) *(tah-kye)*

binbō - kanemochi
(bean-bōh) *(kah-neh-moh-chee)*

quietly - loudly	hot - cold
tall - short	short - long
fast - slow	thick - thin
left - right	above - below
old - young	high - low
poor - rich	inexpensive - expensive

(tah-koo-sahn)   *(soo-koh-shee)*
takusan - sukoshi

(ah-my)   *(soop-pie)*
amai - suppai

(ee-koo-dah)   *(dess)*   *(kah)*
Ikura desu ka?

(oh-gen-kee)   *(dess)*   *(kah)*
Ogenki desu ka?

(wah-tah-shee)
watashi

(wah-tah-shee-tah-chee)
watashitachi

(oh-hi-yōh)   *(goh-zye-mahss)*
ohayō gozaimasu

(oh-yah-soo-mee-nah-sigh)
oyasuminasai

(kohn-nee-chee)   *(wah)*
konnichi wa

(kohn-bahn)   *(wah)*
konban wa

(sigh-yoh-nah-dah)
sayonara

(shee-tsoo-day)
shitsurei

sweet - sour

a lot - a little

How are you?

How much is it?

we

I

good night

good morning

good evening

good day/hello

excuse me

goodbye